# THE TRANS PARENT THREAD:

## ASIAN PHILOSOPHY IN RECENT AMERICAN ART

By

Gail Gelburd

and

Geri De Paoli

**Organized by the Hofstra Museum, Hofstra University
and the Edith C. Blum Art Institute, Bard College**

Distributed by University of Pennsylvania Press

# Tour Itinerary:

Hofstra Museum
Hofstra University
Hempstead, New York
September 16 - November 11, 1990

Edith C. Blum Art Institute
Bard College
Annandale-on-Hudson, New York
December 2, 1990 - February 14, 1991

The Salina Art Center
Salina, Kansas
March 21 - May 23, 1991

Sarah Campbell Blaffer Gallery
University of Houston
Houston, Texas
June 8 - July 28, 1991

Crocker Art Museum
Sacramento, California
September 6 - October 30, 1991

Laguna Art Museum
Laguna Beach, California
November 22, 1991 - February 9, 1992

This exhibition has been funded, in part, by the National Endowment for the Arts, the New York State Council on the Arts and the Edith C. Blum Foundation

LC # 90-084218
ISBN #  cloth: 0-8122-3094-9
        paper: 0-8122-1376-9

© 1990 Hofstra University and Bard College
"Mediations and Humor," © 1990 Geri DePaoli
"Pointing To: The Center of Experience," © 1990  Gail Gelburd

Published by Hofstra University and Bard College.

Distributed by University of Pennsylvania Press, Blockley Hall, 418 Service Drive, Philadelphia, PA 19104

Designed by Jack K. Ruegamer, *Director of Publications, Hofstra University*

# Contents

# Acknowledgments

The merging of opposites is not only an essential component of Eastern philosophy and religious thought, it also characterizes the broader premise of this exhibition: the collaboration between two curators, each concentrating on a particular generation of artists, and the cooperation between two academic institutions—one a large suburban university, the other a small, rural college. It also reflects the lenders, some representing major museums and others, private owners, as well as the artists who practice many extremes of artistic endeavor. The complexity of this venture is, simultaneously, a testimony to its significance. The staff members at the organizing institutions, the lenders, and the artists have each contributed to the explication of this new avenue of art historical inquiry. It is hoped that those who benefit from their efforts will recognize their dedication and their cooperation.

Critical to this collaboration were the tireless dedication and scholarship of co-curator and co-author, Geri De Paoli. The curators and museum directors would like to thank the artists in the exhibition as well as the many others who helped assure the success of the project including Norman Bryson, Betty Cunningham, Julia Gordon, Robert Hannum, Donald Kunitz, Jo Mugnolo, Francis O'Connor, Timothy Rub, Yoshiaki Shimizu, John Skarstad, Elizabeth Turner, Anneke Van Waesberghe and Charles Wright.

We would like to express appreciation to Marci Acita, Karen Becker, and Marilyn Reynolds, Ann Gabler and Judith Samoff at Bard College, and Sou-Ching Chen Lee, Mary Wakeford, Karen Albert, Linda Mondello, M.F. Klerk, Eleanor Rait and Chad Tauber at Hofstra University, to the New York State Council on the Arts, the National Endowment for the Arts and Edith C. Blum Foundation for generously providing partial funding for this project, and to the many lenders who participated. We would like to extend our appreciation to the two institutions which were so supportive of this collaborative effort.

Linda Weintraub, Director, Edith C. Blum Art Institute, Bard College

Dr. Gail Gelburd, Director, Hofstra Museum, Hofstra University

# Preface

Criticism of American art since World War II has continued to use traditional methodologies, placing the art against a backdrop of Western theory rather than acknowledging the shifting perspectives that prevail. The use of traditional Western theory has frequently made the art seem more difficult and inaccessible to the viewer. It seemed to us that there had to be other sources for contemporary art, meanings in the forms, that were not being addressed in the present literature. Working for ten years in opposite parts of the United States, studying different artists and different generations of artists, we arrived independently at the same conclusions—Asian philosophy, particularly Taoism and Zen, had a profound influence on Contemporary American art. A serendipitous meeting almost two years ago led to our collaboration on this project. Our combined efforts reveal a thread that weaves through and ties the art of the last half century together, bridging artists as seemingly diverse as Robert Rauschenberg and Robert Irwin, or John Baldessari and Carl Andre.

Critics have hesitated to address the issue of the influence of Asian concepts either because of their lack of knowledge about them, because they failed to understand the influence, denied its existence, or referred to it as a popular fad. Some have suggested that the alternative world view evidenced by the artists sprang full blown from John Cage or Marcel Duchamp. With additional historical perspective, this text suggests an entirely new philosophical perspective for viewing twentieth century American art.

It must be noted that there are few similarities between Buddhism or Taoism in America and those philosophies in their places of origin—India, China, Japan or South East Asia. What exists in America is American Zen and the American Tao. Indeed the very nature of Buddhism and Taoism demands that when they enter a new culture, they take on the nature of their host. In America, the philosophical experience has been to realign their attitudes about humankind and nature and turn their focus inward.

The text is specifically organized and written to unveil the art in this new context. The reader should keep in mind that the Asian world view is a holistic one in which everything is connected and meanings are carried by the verb. To grasp the essence of the difference between the Occidental and the Oriental perspective one only needs to ponder the term "self-centered." The Asian *Self* refers to the state of awareness of all the connections in the universe – centered, balanced and in harmony in one self while centered in all selves, all others, in nature and the universe. The Western definition of "self-centered" suggests a division between self and others, a negative characteristic. Similarly, interpreting a popular bumper sticker, "Shit Happens" can provide additional insight. In the Occident the emphasis is on the noun, suggesting an unpleasant and derogatory association. In the Orient the emphasis is on the verb and refers to a natural process with no moral or value judgment. Therefore, this manuscript has been written so as to reflect the discourse of Lao Tzu rather than Panofsky. Readers should pause at the italicized words, ponder the spaces between and the paradoxical constructions. The text facilitates the experience of the art.

The introduction to the two essays briefly notes the key sources available to the contemporary American artists since World War II. The sources reach back to the nineteenth century and forward to the writings of D.T. Suzuki and arts of John Cage.

The first essay begins with a review of the cultural climate of the 1950s and 1960s in America followed by an identification of the various means by which Asian ideas were imported. During this period of assimilation of Zen and Tao notions by the artists and by the culture as a whole, eclectic use of the sources led to a philosophical and psychological struggle. The artist's struggle and the art itself is compared with the koan process in Zen Buddhism, one of the potential "paths" to enlightenment. Just as the seeker of enlightenment is given a "koan" (a paradoxical question) to ponder, the artist presents the issues of reality and illusion which the viewer must transcend. This essay presents an alternative perspective from which to view Funk, Pop, Happenings and Performance Art and shows the art to be more readily accessible through the overlay of the Asian world view.

Changes are recorded in the intent, process and product of the American artist, as well as a change in the very reason for making art and in expectations on the part of each viewer. This essay is intended to present a conceptual framework from which to consider all of the art that follows this shift in world view. It emphasizes that the few artists chosen represent the many.

The next essay focuses on the art of the 1970s. The historical and political events of the period demonstrate the increased exposure that Americans had to the Asian world view. South East Asia, its problems and ideologies became an integral part of daily life. Artists were particularly attuned to the philosophies and reflect the concepts in their art. The artists read about East Asia, read the texts and became increasingly sophisticated about philosophical sources from Wittgenstein to Lao Tzu.

This essay uses the art itself to explicate that the influence was, by the 1970s, pervasive. The works chosen are examples which could be easily substituted for other works by the same artist or by other artists of the period. Each artist came to these Asian concepts via various routes, and many of them shared their perceptions with each other. They experimented with a wide range of art forms (earth, light, sound, film, space) in order to find expression for this non-Western world view. It is the concepts addressed in the works that are the constant. While the first essay analyzes the work of artists who were struggling to see the ideas, the second essay discusses the artists whose work directs the viewer (turned participant) to a centering experience. The works used as examples in the second essay address the idea of balancing opposing forces and yet finding an inner harmony; they are about directing the viewer to an inward experience of the art; to make the viewer a participant of an art that is not necessarily on the outside but centered inside of the viewer/participant.

The next section of text provides the reader with additional visual examples accompanied by relevant commentary and biography on each artist. Arranged alphabetically rather than chronologically, the comparisons can be easily made. The bibliography which follows should be seen as a research tool for future studies on the subject but in no way is meant to be an all-inclusive list. The book ends with an abridged glossary for quick and easy access to terms that might not be familiar to the reader.

The question of whether American Buddhism or the artists' idiosyncratic use of Zen or Tao material is authentic is not the issue in this book. Instead it asks what American artists took from the volumes of Buddhist and Tao material, how they used it, and what were the long term consequences? The artists came in contact with various types of Asian materials, both formal and philosophical, and the fact is that critics and art historians have not addressed this influence adequately. The material in this book is put forth in the spirit of all beginnings, with the knowledge that it may contain some oversights and simplifications. The book does not analyze the art before World War II which was influenced by Asian philosophy, nor does it discuss European artists or even all of the contemporary American artists that might be included in this study. Rather, it is the hope that what is presented here will greatly encourage needed studies in the future.

GG and GDP, August 1990

Fig. 1. John Cage, *Where R=Ryoanji 12 R/13 - 3/90*  March 1990
Pencil on handmade paper
10 x 19"
Courtesy Margarete Roeder Gallery

# Introduction

*One can tell for oneself whether the water is warm or cold. In the same way,*
*a man must convince himself about these experiences, then only are they real.*
I-Ching

In the course of human existence, at different stages along *the path*, individuals have searched for their *true self*. To understand the nature of existence and the relevance of one's place in the universe has been a quest since before the discipline of philosophy was named. As the world becomes increasingly technological and complex, we speak of *simplifying* -- finding a *way* that can help distinguish "hot from cold" *illusion* from *reality*. Facing this dilemma, artists, writers, poets, and philosophers from the studios and the streets of the Occident have looked to the Orient for answers and alternative perspectives. Many have found the source for exploration and an alternative perspective in Taoism and Buddhism, in the *Tao Te Ching* and the *I-Ching*, in the *Lotus Sutra* and *Tibetan Book of the Dead,* as well as in the interpretations of modern philosphers such as D. T. Suzuki or Alan Watts. The artists in this study, as well as many others, were and continue to be profoundly affected by the art and ideas of Asia.

Japanese prints, ceramics, scroll paintings and architecture have provided Western artists with an alternative aesthetic influence. However, it is the philosophical ideas of Taoism and Zen Buddhism, in particular, that have had the greatest impact on the artists of the last half of the twentieth century. They saw the aesthetics of the Far East in the works of Eduard Manet, Georgia O'Keeffe, and Mark Tobey, but they sought to go beyond the surface of the forms to understand the power that conceived the aesthetics. The artists were predisposed to exploration, and to an interior journey, from the

art they saw and their readings of Western philosophers such as Wittgenstein or Mallarmé. The works they made function as traces of their journey and there is irrefutable evidence that the map they used led to Asia. The text that follows points the way to experiencing the inner meanings of much of contemporary art.

The journey toward inner exploration began over one hundred years ago when Ralph Waldo Emerson and Walt Whitman were reading the *Bhagavad Gita* (the great book of thought from India), and Henry David Thoreau was writing that he sought "... to realize his Self, directing his eye right inward, and to find a thousand regions in his mind yet undiscovered." At this time Buddhists began to migrate to America, and Americans such as John La Farge and Ernst Fenollosa journeyed to Japan. Philosophical thought derived from the Orient stimulated the artists.

Contact with Asia after World War II through Korea and Vietnam, Laos and Cambodia renewed the connections and artists were particularly sensitive to holistic Asian ideas.

Michael Sullivan wrote in the pioneering study, *The Meeting of Eastern and Western Art* (1973), "... East and West have traditionally felt differently about the world and have expressed their feelings in very different ways. Only when we realize how great these differences are, can we fully appreciate the achievement of the creative artists." The impact of East Asia on contemporary American culture has now become apparent at all levels. It can

Fig. 2. John Cage, *New River Watercolor Series II* 1988
Watercolor on paper
26 x 72"
Courtesy Margarete Roeder Gallery

be seen not only in literature, music, film and visual art, but also in television, cuisine, medicine and automobiles.

Contemporary artists began to investigate the inherent differences. Their work, as well as their own words, reveal their sources. The sources most frequently mentioned are the *Tao Te Ching*, the *I-Ching*,and the interpretations of Zen provided by D.T. Suzuki, and Alan Watts. Other artists have mentioned the *Lotus Sutra*, the *Tibetan Book of the Dead*, the writings of Christmas Humphreys, the Beat writers, Pirsig's *Zen and the Art of Motorcycle Maintenance*, writings of Mallarmé or Merleau Ponty and Herrigel's *Zen and the Art of Archery*.

The *I-Ching* (Book of Changes),which reiterates Buddhist and Taoist notions, was a pervasive tool amongst artists. "*I*" means change, easy, understated."Ching" is the unchangeable. The message is one of flux, randomness and openness to all possibilities. The *Tao Te Ching* is a classic manual for the art of living. Chinese wisdom is conveyed through the eighty-one statements contained in the book.

D. T. Suzuki, who wrote volumes on Zen Buddhism, made public appearances and gave lectures, was a powerful presence in the United States until his death in 1966. He wrote in a succinct and clear format how Zen was incorporated into a rock garden or *sumi* painting, the martial arts or psychotherapy. Suzuki was known to the artists, writers and musicians as the guide to understanding the concepts behind the forms.

Alan Watts has been referred to as the popularizer of Zen; however, a majority of the artists who came of age in the 1950s, and were mentors to the next generation, came to Taoism and Zen directly through Alan Watts' writings, lectures and radio program. David

Hockney stated in a recent interview," When I came to this country in the 1960s, Alan Watts was a father figure to a lot of artists I met. They followed him around like puppy dogs."[1] Zen and Tao, in fact, collapse hierarchies between high and low, academic and popular. In America these ideas have been attractive precisely because they are linked to our democratic values. It is important to realize that many changes in attitudes, and in art, which come about as a result of the assimilation of Asian influence came about by way of popular interpretations of those ideas and not directly from the primary sources. Asian sources have been mixed with Western disciplines to gain new insights and perspectives. This can be seen, for example, in Alan Watts' book *Psychotherapy East and West*, or Fritjof Capra's *Tao of Physics*. Similarly, the Beat poets, notably Jack Kerouac, Allen Ginsberg and Gary Snyder served as popular interpreters of Zen and Tao. The new world view is an American Zen and an American Tao — a transformation and mutation from their origin.

John Cage, musician, poet and artist, transformed the Tao, Zen, in his modern music. As a student of D.T. Suzuki he interpreted the ideas as well as those of the *I-Ching* to others. Cage sat in Suzuki's class and meditated with him. "All my life when I needed a teacher, one arrived," stated Cage in a recent interview. He described Suzuki's class and explained, that "Suzuki would walk into the classroom with a brisk athletic feeling ( despite his age). He took a book that he had tied with silk and unwrapped it and put it aside. Finally he would find something that interested him."[2] Cage also went to hear Watts speak but emphasizes that for him Suzuki was the real teacher. John Cage believes that Suzuki helped him to see music,

Fig. 3. John Cage, *No. 2, 4/12/90* April 1990
Fire and watercolor on paper
26 1/2 x 39 1/2"
Courtesy Margarete Roeder Gallery

...not as a communication from artist to audience, but rather as an activity of sounds in which the artist found a way to let the sounds be themselves. Sounds which could open the minds of the people who made them or listened to them, to other possibilities than they had previously considered ... to widen their experience; particularly to undermine the making of value judgements.

The testing of art by means of life, stated Cage, " was the result of attending the lectures of Suzuki for three years."[3]

Cage has been a critical link between the Far East and the American artists. He was decisive in cultivating an atmosphere and a sensibility that influenced composers, choreographers, painters and sculptors. He became one of the key figures in the arts of the 1950s and 1960s and continues to be considered a mentor to many today. As a musician he programmed sounds to produce an experience which simulated the random noises we hear in life. Called "chance" compositions or "chaotic," they are ordered disorder. His recent visual art "burn pieces" are monotypes in which he has burned the paper to create an arbitrary, uncontrolled circular image (fig.3). His *Ryoan-ji* drawings and watercolors are based on the great rock garden in Japan but are literally tracings of the rocks he collects in his studio. Tracing the rocks, he has found that he organizes the random experience (fig.1,2).

Cage and many other poets, writers and artists have assimilated Asian philosophical attitudes and transformed them in their art in new and exciting ways. Similarly other artists such as Mark Tobey, Morris Graves, Ad Reinhardt, Clyford Still, and Barnett Newman presented these ideas to their disciples, and the disciples of their disciples. The examination of, and experimentation with Asian notions, forms and practices resulted in a re-examination of fundamental elements and relationships. The encounter with Asian ideas resulted in new ways of seeing, new ways of being, new conceptions, and new experiences of space, time, form, void, subject, and the object.

The artists came to understand the concepts and Asian terms that explicate the differences between

Eastern and Western perspectives. (A glossary at the end of the book defines the terms.) The essence of life, *chi* for example, is usually translated as "life breath" or "spirit resonance." *Yin-Yang* refers to the complementary nature of pairs of dualities; in Western languages these opposites could be man/woman, active/passive, day/night, black/white, up/down. In Asian thought these dualities collapse and lead to cooperation rather than competition. *Tai Chi* is the activity of balancing the *Yin-Yang*. The *Tao* is translated as "path" or "way" and the symbol for it is water, which can not be held but is the strongest of all elements, capable of carving stone. "Go with the flow" is a Taoist phrase. A critical aspect of the *Tao Te Ching* (Way of Life) is *wu-wei*, (doing-not doing) and for the artist means allowing the inspiration to occur. The paradox of apparent opposites (wu-wei , I-Ching, doing-not doing) appears also in the unanswerable questions posed by a *koan*. A common *"koan,"* which frequently contains humor, is " what is the sound of one hand clapping?" or "At midnight, in Silla, the sun is shining." These are statements given to the seeker of enlightenment from his or her master. The *koan* is a paradoxical statement that leads the disciple beyond thought, beyond reason, beyond the illusion of dualities. There is no logical answer to the *koan* yet its consideration leads to a shift in perspective and a new awareness.

The Asian concept of self is also radically different. The "self" is a manifestation of ego. Power from the Asian view comes from balance, from the spaces in between from the force behind. There is no imposition of an order, a form or an ego. Absence of "ego" in Asian philosophy does not connote a state of emptiness but a transcendent state of "fullness" and vision. The Buddhist concept of emptiness has been a compelling notion for artists from the 1950s to the present. Emptiness or the void is a dynamic field of energy, empty and full of limitless possibilities. It is Pu, the Uncarved Block, form laden with potential. Lao Tzu expresses the idea most profoundly .....

Thirty spokes will converge
In the hub of a wheel
But the use of the cart
Will depend on the part
of the hub that is void

So advantage is had
From whatever is there;
But usefulness rises
From whatever is not.

— Lao Tzu

As contemporary artists became aware of these various concepts, their perceptions of space was reordered as an active void, an ocean of possibilities waiting to be recognized. Rejecting the idea of linear progress along with linear perspective and the hierarchical order of society and art, the artist realized that they were a part of nature. No fixed conclusions or absolute judgments were possible within this new world view. It required a suspension of judgment and abandonment of prejudice to find the secrets of art and existence.

In East Asia the secrets of the essence of life are written into the Sutras, books of wisdom. The knowledge and attitudes they contain are incorporated into the very fabric of the culture and society. But Sutra translated literally means "thread" and it is this "thread" of knowing which we will trace through the art of the last half century. At times the thread may seem transparent but its presence is everpresent—structuring the forms, embodying the spirit. If the reader, now participant, proceeds with a clear mind, open to experience and change, the Trans parent Thread will glisten.

Gail Gelburd
Geri DePaoli

1. Interview between Geri DePaoli and David Hockney, 1985.
2. Interview between John Cage and Gail Gelburd, 1990.
3. Kostelanetz, *John Cage*.

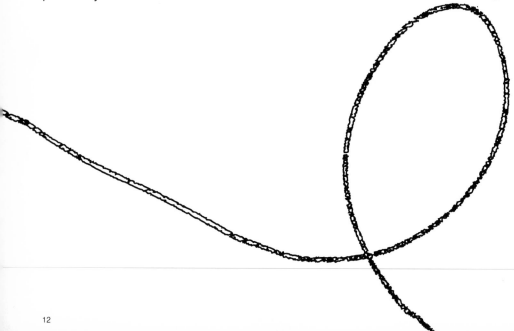

13

# Meditations and Humor: Art as Koan

Geri DePaoli

From early in this century material from the Far East has continued to add patches to the multicolored quilt that is American culture.  Additions of various shapes and sizes have followed Asian-American contacts during World War II, the wars in Korea and Vietnam, and the more recent economic associations with Japan. Various Asian  patterns have given texture and color to American art and culture yet  the origin of these designs, some obvious, some subtle, has been obscured and can only  become clearly visible once the quilt is turned and its connecting threads examined.

Because cultural interpretations have focused on individual segments of  the pattern,  and not on the whole, the pervasive presence of Asian ideas and practices among the literati of the 1950s and in the popular culture of the 1960s has been dismissed as a fad.  Taisen Deshimaru comments:

> Isn't Zen becoming a fad?  What does that matter?  A fad is a response to a need but it does not last.  To endure a practice demands effort and perseverance There are always people who understand and continue beyond passing fads and fashion.  The fad leaves something behind.  The wave ebbs but the ocean remains.[1]

This essay will address the fact that the lives and works of American artists from the 1940s through the 1960s have been greatly affected by contacts with Asian art and ideas and it will point to the profound impact that remains long after the fad.[2]

Long before the 1940s, as Rick Fields points out in his history of *Buddhism in America*, elements of Asian aesthetics and philosophy contributed to American art and culture.[3] In fact,  from the beginning of the century Asian forms and ideas have gradually been assimilated into American culture and have made up the fiber of  a transparent thread.  Tracing this thread allows for a revised and simplified view of American art  which clarifies complexities and shows it  to be more of  a continuum rather than a series of disparate "isms."

Initially, art and ideas from Asia produced the phenomena known as japonisme and chinoiserie.  Collectors,  as well as the common householder, had a passion for "orientalia."  The fascination with the art was with the decorative and design quality especially in ceramics, textiles and prints. The pathway of ideas also began in  the 18th century when translations of the *Bhagavad Gita*, Taoist and Buddhist writings offered an alternative world view to the Western hierarchical political, social and spiritual order.

These mystical and  philosophical  notions were at first received with a Romantic sensibility;  the interest was in the exotic and mysterious nature of the Orient and in the quality of the picturesque.   A few American artists and writers nevertheless began to assimilate the ideas and in the process began to alter their world view. The residue of early interest in Asian thought can be seen in American transcendental and nature literature.[4]

American consciousness was deeply stirred when Swami Vivekananda and Soyen Shaku spoke at the World Religions Pavilion in Chicago in 1893. Their ideas generated such interest that explorations of Asian philosophy and practices increased exponentially and changed in character. What once had seemed exotic, strange and incomprehensible began to be incorporated into American religious, philosophical and artistic expressions. Early Modernist attitudes dealing with wholeness, unity, and non-hierarchical ways were fertilized by Buddhist, Tao and Hindu writings.[5]

Publications and programs of the American Theosophical Society and writings of Pound, Emerson, Thoreau,Whitman and Carl Jung served as vehicles for transmitting aspects of the Asian world view through many levels of American culture. The literati began to consider this way of thinking, especially the Asian holistic attitude toward nature, as a serious alternative to European Romanticism and Rationalism.[6] The new notions from Asia generated a provocative and powerful force. Assimilated and mutated over time they became so deeply ingrained in our own sense of our culture that in most instances the depth and significance of the Oriental influence on American art and culture passed unnoted by critics and commentators. Perhaps because the philosophy was compatible with the American intuition about human nature , the ideas already seemed our own.[7]

Yet today many Americans, including art historians and critics, continue to consider Asian influence with a Romantic sensibility. They expect work influenced by the Orient to look like Oriental art. This is not necessarily the case. Instead it is the assimilation of Asian thought that has had a great impact on American art and consciousness; it has, in fact, contributed to "a shifting cultural paradigm."[8] Art criticism suffers from previous failures to mark those qualities which came originally from the Orient. The neglect of Asian influence has led to needless complexity and confusion in the interpretation of much 20th-century American art. Critics have searched painfully for explanations from within the Western tradition of logic and reason. John Baldessari says that the Asian way of thinking simply gives Americans permission to be themselves and to be American.[9]

The nature, character, and mechanisms of early 20th-century influences need to be explored further and that examination is sure to enhance and, in some cases, revise some of the interpretation of that art. Asian influence was indeed present though not often noted.[10] The task here, however, is to look at the patterns of Asian influence in the 1950s and 1960s and consider their impact on the intent, process and product of the artist and on the role of the viewer / participant. [11] Changes for the artist include new attitudes about space, time, form, void, subject and object as well as new conceptions about the very reason for making art. For the viewer there is a change in how art is experienced.

# Cultural Patterns

In the 1950's a simmering dissatisfaction with "sin and science" as a model for Western cultural response began to crystallize. Sociologist Robert Janes has said that without the concept of sin, where nature is to be tamed, the west would not have developed science, the manipulation and control of nature.[12] Avant-garde poets, writers, musicians and visual artists began to re-examine attitudes about sin and science, about human relationships and nature. Among fundamental concepts considered by the literati were the Judeo-Christian notion that nature was considered to be separate from, and designed for the use of, humankind and the idea of a hierarchical relationship between individuals.

Alternative ways of thinking were considered. European proposals from psychotherapy to Existentialism were explored, parts integrated, but much rejected as too pessimistic. Asian thought, in the form it was offered, was found to be compatible with the American character. It was non-hierarchical and insisted on direct experience with nature, was non-literary and affirmed the rugged individual. These perceptions should now be set within the context of 1950s and 1960s America.

The following list of phenomena and people can serve to distill the essence of that era. The 1950s were marked by the Korean War, the Eisenhower years, the Mc Carthy hearings, the "establishment," the military-industrial complex, the generation gap, Jack Kerouac, Beatniks, cosmic consciousness, Marilyn Monroe, James Dean and Elvis Presley. The 1960s resonate with assassinations, the civil rights movement, Vietnam, peace marches, hippies, gurus, the Beatles, Jane Fonda, Joan Baez, Pop art.

In the 1950s and 1960s writings by D.T. Suzuki, Richard Wilhelm, Eugen Herrigel, Joseph Campbell, Paul Reps and Alan Watts were doors to Asian influence since they contained translations from original Asian writings as well as popular interpretations. The music and performance of John Cage, the poetry of the Beats, and the writings of J.D. Salinger all helped to Americanize these notions. By the 1960s Asian influence appeared in popular culture in the music of the Beatles, the practice of martial arts, a developed adaptation of the Japanese aesthetic in ceramics, architecture and evidence of Asian design in contemporary fashion .[13] At this time American art and culture were informed by aspects of an Asian world view which led to the re-definition of the individual, the (re)placement of the ego (not substituted but given less importance) and the re-evaluation of the macho nature of American culture.

Other patterns of thought from Asian sources, which filtered into American intellectual consciousness, included de-centering the sacred, rejection of absolute value judgments, acceptance of paradox, recognition of the Yin-Yang (relativism), a trust in chance or randomness, and a notion of cyclical processes rather than a linear idea of progress. [14]

Fig. 4. William Wiley, *Slant Step MCMLXVI* 1966
Cast concrete with metal chain
24 1/2 x 13 x 14 1/2" and 41 1/2"
Oakland Museum, Art Division

Consequences of the assimilation of Asian conceptions by artists in the 1950s and 1960s can be articulated by the phrase, " from metaphor to suchness." Art was no longer considered a substitute for or referent to something in the visible world. No outside model existed by which one could measure the work. Artists chose mechanisms of meditation and humor whereby they placed the viewer/participant within a framework of experience. Works of art were considered to be mirrors in which the viewer could see through to the "Self." The intent was to achieve a new perspective or an altered awareness of a dynamic network of connections.

The following group of quotations serve to demonstrate the diverse mechanisms of influence and diverse responses as well as to establish the pervasive presence of material from Zen Buddhism and Taoism. (The type of Buddhism called Zen from Japan was first Chan in China where it took on its character by being overlaid with the mystical ideas and attitudes of the Tao, the mystical Chinese texts of legendary Lao Tzu and Chuang Tzu. The Zen/Tao transmission to America resulted in altered or mutant forms which have notably American characteristics.)

Many artists made comparisons between the Zen/Tao material and traditional western thought and practice.

> ...the grain of [classical Western] thinking
> was measured, rational intellectual; it had

prospered in a hothouse fertilized by Aristotle, not life. It was a paralyzing heritage... I never understood I was a prisoner until I was freed and I didn't know I was free until long after it happened.
The road to myself had to be subversive and indebted to chance... I met John Cage in Rockland County in 1954. We had a house, a piano, books, booze and time....John laughed at the tales of his own unhappiness, failures, tries, mocking audiences...and finding a way, Zen. And mushrooms, koan; I resisted it all, I still do. But I was changed. A frail enlightenment came to a materialist....Without John, I never would have been able to make 'Point of Order' many years later. Without John, I wouldn't be writing these words. In his Zen I found America. Also, that art is what artists do.
(Emile de Antonio from published version of the film "Painters Painting.")

It was in the 50's that John Cage brought Zen downtown. He gave his lectures on 'something' and 'nothing.' Then everyone seemed to be reading Suzuki, and later Alan Watts. They didn't talk about it, they acted. There was a feeling at the Club [Artists Club in New York] ...that somewhere there were two people who would sort of walk by each other early in the morning and nod to one another and all knowledge would pass between them... There was also an attitude toward discursive exposition, it wasn't the thing to do.
(John Loftus , Hobart and William Smith-Colleges, interview with the author.)

Beat Zen is a complex phenomenon. It ranges from a use of Zen for justifying sheer caprice in art, literature and life to a very forceful social criticism and 'digging the universe' such as one may find in the poetry of Ginsberg and Snyder and rather unevenly in Kerouac...I see no real quarrel with either extreme. There was never a spiritual movement without its excesses and distortions.
(Alan Watts, Chicago Review , Summer 1958 Bulletin 12 p8-9.)

Let me say that since 1948 up until now, and now more than ever, my reading of Zen has been intense. The ideas expressed by Suzuki have always been an ideal for me in painting.
(Phillip Guston, 1979 statement quoted in David Clarke.)

Yes, those ideas [Zen] were around, everywhere, you could accept it or reject it. Some artists took it in totally and pursued it, made it part of themselves, like Tobey, Reinhardt and even Barney Newman, Some took parts of it and others rejected it. You can see the difference on the surface and in the edges, the Eastern work is contemplative, in the West they still need the angst to spark the creativity.
(Aaron Siskind , interview with the author.)

I read the Asian material early, Suzuki, Watts, Herrigel. and I took a course in Chinese art. It seemed that the ideas were compatible with the American nature; the humor, the attitude toward nature. In Oriental art they're more comfortable with humor, there is no real humor in Western art. For me Godzilla movies

demonstrate Eastern thought, he is an element of nature not an evil monster.
(John Baldessari, 1989 interview with the author.)

First, isn't Zen everywhere...? It's a way of seeing, being. For me it was introduced when I lived in Washington State, near the first atomic plant. The East has a different attitude toward nature. And in art an influence would be Duchamp, for me Duchamp was Zen.
(William T. Wiley, interview with the author.)

Yes, Zen ideas were around in the 50's and 60's, I guess the ideas kind of became part of us. I often listened to Alan Watts' radio programs about Zen while I worked in my studio. Many artists did, and still do. His recordings are still played on KPFA in San Francisco."
(Wayne Theibaud, interview with the author.)

"I first came to Asian thought through Bernard Leach, 'The Art of the Potter.' Then Alan Watts , he had a radio program in the 60's, it's still going, Now I listen in the most proper way, background noise, but of course you still listen.
(Robert Arneson, interview with the author.)

After a move to Arizona from New York, and my first real experience with emptiness, it matched my poetic readings and the Oriental notion of filled and unfilled...I spent a lot of time reading about Oriental thought, mostly Suzuki. ...and I have given away over five hundred copies of Herrigel's 'Zen and the Art of Archery.' Also some pathways opened through Alan Watts and the Beat Generation...particularly Kerouac, he Americanized those experiences for me.
(Harvey Himelfarb, University of California at , Davis, interview with the author.)

The mind of western man, by means of science, is being led inevitably towards a meeting with the no-mind of the pure Zen Buddhist doctrine of the Orient.
(R. Lippold, "To Make Love to Life," *College Art Journal, Summer* 1960 p. 303.)

In the 1950s and 1960s transformed attitudes and practices among artists, writers and musicians led to a more clearly definable American culture and art which was no longer totally derived from Europe. Far Eastern ideas and practices were matched with Existential and psychoanalytic theories and the Asian ideas proved to be a catalyst in a new cultural precipitate. Those who were sympathetic to the Far Eastern conceptions and those who were unsympathetic to them were all affected by the entry of this alternative philosophy into the American mind . We can gauge the consequences of the impact on American artists by observing altered attitudes, motivation, and practices which reflect an altered consciousness.[15]

A modification of the world view of many artists occurred in concert with uniquely American political, economic and cultural patterns that emerged as a result of a series of estrangements and re-evaluations. In the wake of World War II, America found itself ministering to its former European mentor. The perception of a loss of European leadership and America's assumption of a new position of power within the international community contributed to a re-examination of motives and goals. Within the cauldron of Cold War politics, stirred by the exponential growth of the mass media, American identity crystallized in a network of paradox.

Among the literati, many of the tried and true Western values and assumptions were questioned; by the late 1950s everything was fair game, from the existence of God to the nature of matter.[16] For many artists and writers, a conceptual journey from Descartes to Newton to Einstein (from absolutes to relativity) was paralleled by ideas from the I- Ching, the Tao and Zen Buddhism. For many the nihilist Existential path seemed less compatible with their experience. However, some of the artists mention Heidegger, Merleau-Ponty and the late writing of Wittgenstein as expressing notions they found similar to the Buddhist world view.[17]

In the midst of personal philosophical explorations, universities spawned departments of "American Studies" as they later would develop "Women's Studies" and "Oriental Studies," suggesting that a recognizable entity existed that allowed for naming and analysis. The era was marked by a mix of affluence and the beginnings of alienation. The co-existence of value systems of the Eisenhower administration and its celebration of technology with the "Beat" generation and its radically different attitudes towards politics and material goods became known as the "generation gap"; it was philosophical not chronological. The terms beatnik, egghead, square, establishment and pig, followed by hippie, pot head, flower children and peaceniks, euphemistically identified the philosophical separations in the culture.

At first Norman Mailer's voice of dissent from the conformist literary establishment was a cry in the wilderness. But soon many writers and artists labeled themselves anti-establishment or non-comformist, partially in response to the McCarthyite political repression that was felt at every level of society. The "establishment" was defined as a power structure that exploited the common man and raped the environment in an uninhibited attempt to secure power and to gain wealth. Its morality was Calvinist, which assigned status to the possession of worldly goods and valued "usefulness" in its art objects.

Visible in the genesis and birth of anti-establishment values were the seeds of new attitudes about human rights, ecological consciousness and anti-materialism, which were to burst forth into popular culture in the 1960s. Ideas circulating from writings on Zen and Tao sometimes generated, sometimes validated, an evolving value system. Human rights became an issue when confidence in the rightness of the "American way" was shaken by the experience of the McCarthy hearings. The widely felt confidence in the process of government was shaken. The very processes of judgment itself were questioned as well as the

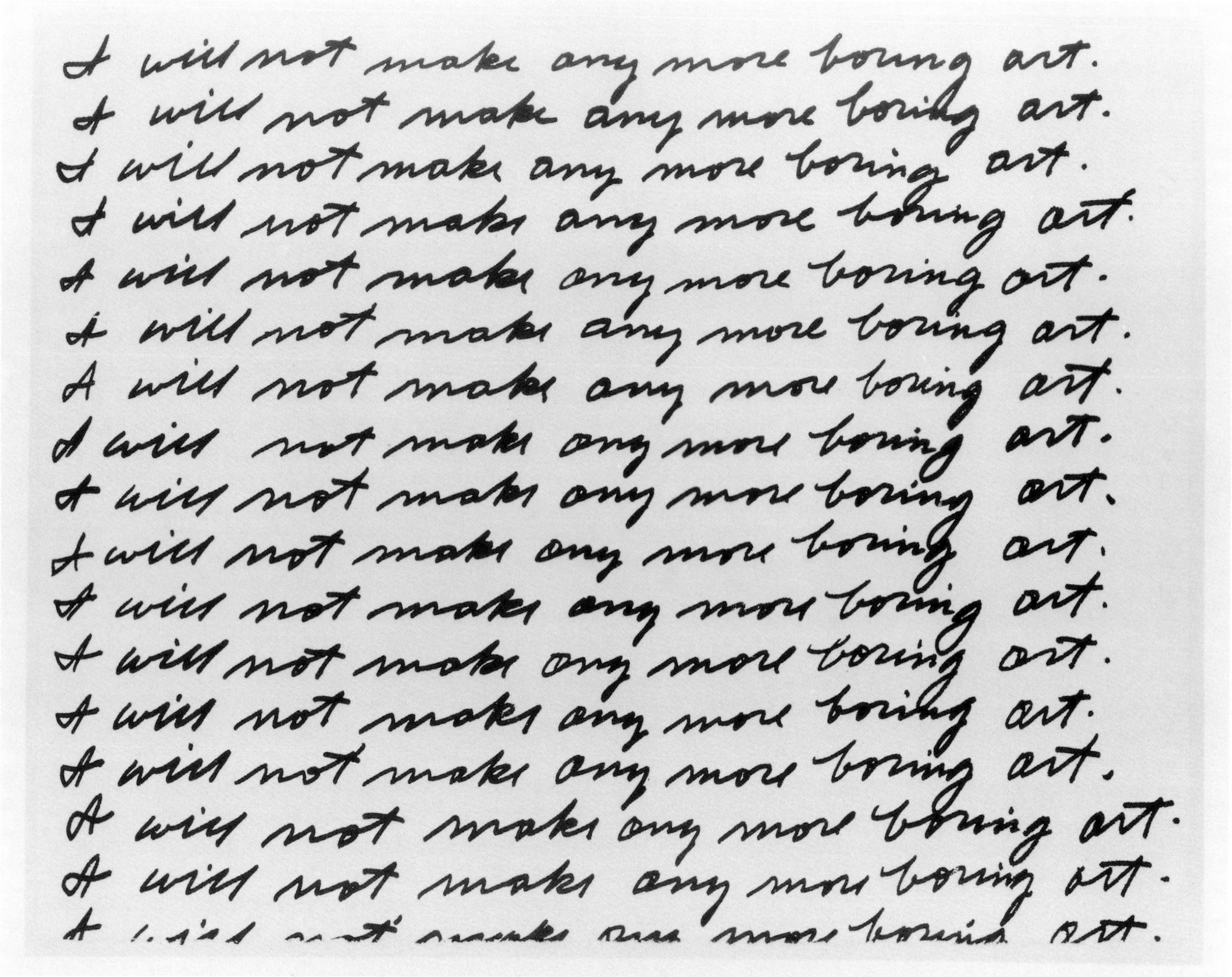

Fig. 5. John Baldessari, *I Will Not Make Any More Boring Art* 1971
Lithograph, printed in black
22 1/8 x 29 9/16"
The Museum of Modern Art, New York,
John B. Turner Fund

idea of absolutes in the social, physical and psychological world.

Relativistic notions from Zen/Tao material stated the impossibility of fixed judgments or human hierarchies; less hierarchical ways were sought. In addition the Asian holistic attitude toward nature and the use of the female nature as a metaphor for the Tao, were seminal to a rising consciousness of ecology, civil rights and a new awareness of the role of women. Martin Luther King, Jr., who patterned himself after Ghandi, subscribed to the alternative set of values and emphasized the attitude of non-violence.[18]

Transformations were especially telling within the 'Beat' generation, where, as a direct result of their interpetation and assimilation of Far Eastern thinking, dualisims collapsed and former opposites became complements. Good and bad, up and down, now and then, were relative to each other and to context. These artists and writers were actually mapping a new culture.[19] Baldessari very clearly articulates the issue (fig. 5).

I had read other sources on Oriental thinking earlier but the Beats Americanized the ideas of the Far East for me; they popularized it. It was the kind of leveling that attracted me, no one thing more important than another.
John Baldessari

So while within the establishment the post-War American had played the role of the man on the white horse, wearing a white hat, heroically preserving American democracy for the world, in another segment of society named anti-establishment, a hierarchical order of authority or a deterministic value system was no longer accepted. Jack Kerouac's "On the Road" presented an alternative picture of the American hero, and many people from San Francisco to Chicago to New York became "Dharma Bums."

As with any shift in cultural paradigm, divisions became sharper and power centers became defensive and resistant to change. Estrangements led to new meanings for previously named groups and institutions. Gaps developed between intellectuals and government, science and art, artists and the public. The academic community, which had given a favorable rating to the government now turned to criticism; non-conformists considered the leadership to have gone astray in service of the military-industrial complex. The "establishment" considered the Beats and the hippies to be somewhere between subversive and irrelevant.

In further realignments, visual artists', poets' and writers' pursuits were perceived by the public as of little value when compared to the technological wonders produced by the scientists. Science was considered as that course of study which would benefit society directly by the creation of products to improve the quality of life. By the 1960s, as a partial result of this rift between art and science, a new thought pattern was constructed, "legitimization by association." The process began with the collapse of economic support for artists by government agencies ( e.g. WPA), and the rapid expansion of departments of art within universities replacing the apprentice system or art school training.

Since such high value was placed upon science within the university, funds were more available for scientific proposals. Many administrators within all divisions of the humanities began to define their pursuits by using scientific discourse. The practice had far- reaching consequences, especially in the content and language of art criticism. This type of discourse flowed back to the artists and critics and affected the way in which they defined themselves. Artists and art historians tried to sound like scientists and avoided any associations with mysticism or spirituality.

While within colleges and universities the study and practice of art and the study of Asian thought were legitimized by association with scientific disciplines (psychology and physics), estrangements grew between the public and the intellectual and artistic communities.[20] Now more than ever the general public perceived artists as eccentric and unproductive. Early in the decade "modern" artists had been alienated not only from society but also from a part of their own artistic community. Within this hostile atmosphere, these artists found the Zen/Tao philosophy positive and attractive with its descriptions of the unconventional "sage" and the permission to simply "be." [21]

By mid-fifties new relationships emerged for artists who were labled "modern." Depending upon the segment of society assigning value, artists' status ranged from "guru" to "weirdo." Many artists, behaving like "'Zen men" (or women, although they were few), described their mission to paint, sculpt, print, to "be" in the Zen/Tao sense. They followed the Zen dictum to find their own nature, and they perceived that nature to be "artist" and "American."[22] They no longer sought the approval of the establishment.

A representative articulation of non-conformist thinking and its rejection of absolute judgments can be found in a popular translation of the Tao Te Ch'ing.

People through finding something beautiful
Think something else unbeautiful,
Through finding one man fit
Judge another unfit.
Life and death, though stemming from each other
Seem to conflict as stages of change,
Difficult and easy as phases of achievement,
Long and short as measures of contrast,
High and low as degrees of relation;
But since the varying of tones gives music to a voice and what is is the was of what shall be,
The sanest man
Sets up no deed,
Lays down no law,
Takes everything that happens as it comes,
As something to animate, not to appropriate,
To earn, not to own,
To accept naturally without self-importance:
If you never assume importance you never lose it.

(From The Way of Life According to Lao Tzu Witter Bynner.)

In the '60's many artists found their attitude toward language compatible with another often quoted expression from the *Tao Te Ching*. (They also compared this attitude to contemporary French writings on semiotics and linguistics.)

There are ways but the way is uncharted;
There are names but not nature in words:
Nameless indeed is the source of creation
But things have a mother and she has a name.
The secret waits for the insight
Of eyes unclouded by longing;
Those who are bound by desire
See only the outward container.

Translation by R.B. Blakney

A re-examination of artists' statements in light of Far Eastern ideas yields numerous code words for Tao/ Buddhist conceptions. For example, J.D. Salinger encapsulized Asian notions by direct and indirect references to Buddhism and Taoism.[23] In the following phrases from his 1955 "Franny and Zooey," he used Buddhist code words.

"Detachment, buddy, and only detachment. Desirelessness. Cessation from all hankerings...in one damn incarnation or another, if you like- -you not only had a hankering to be an actor or an actress but to be a good one. You're stuck with it now. You can't just walk out on the results of your own hankerings...The only thing you can do now, the only religious thing you can do, is act." This scene carries the Buddhist sense of ultimate responsibility coming from the Self: finding one's own nature and following the direction from within (permission). No guidance is sought from an outside source as a God or social law. [24]

Echoing the spirit of Salinger's Buddhist morality, in the visual arts, artists found their direction from within themselves. And in the holistic spirit they trusted that the most personal expression would be a universal ex-

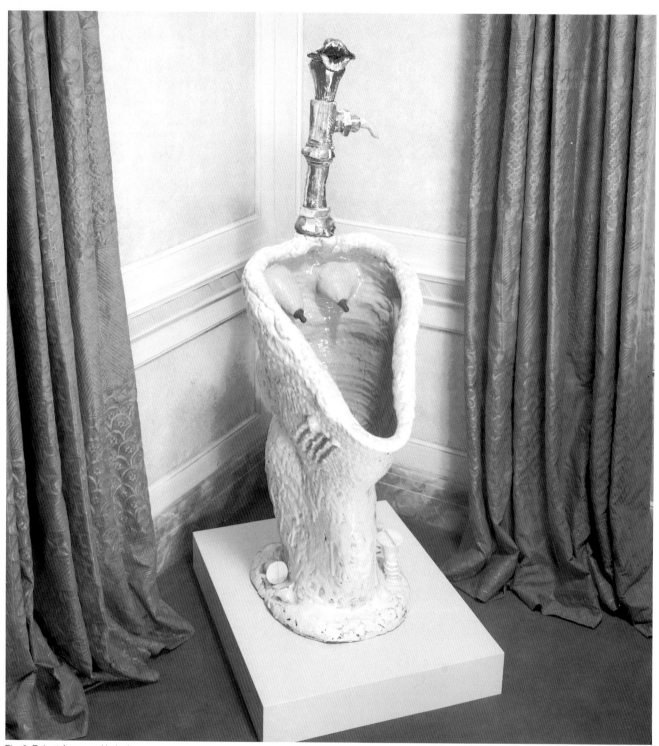

Fig. 6. Robert Arneson, *Herinal*
ceramic
49" x 16" x 20" (without base)
Jederman Collection, N.A.

pression because they were connected. The art of ex-
pressionistic abstraction can be understood as an art of
meditation (a way to knowledge) or as a mandala (the
cosmic diagram of the universe in which the meditator is
centered.) Both deal with transcending visible reality.
Problems with space, form, void and the notion of process were of prime concern in the art that did not deal

with objects from the visible world. In a group of etchings called, *A Suite of Daze*, (fig. 7-10) William Wiley expressed his concerns. Opposite one of the etchings he
included a statement after a work which addressed the
interrelationship of form and void, " Form is void, void is
form, form is void, void is form but when all is said and
done Norm is really Lloyd." He used Zen humor which

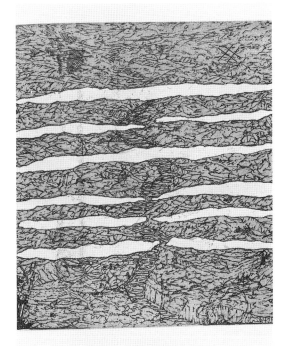

### ⅀ Chin / Progress ⅀

The hexagram represents the sun rising over the earth. It is therefore the symbol of rapid, easy progress, which at the same time means ever widening expansion and clarity.

*The Judgment*

PROGRESS. The powerful prince
Is honored with horses in large numbers.
In a single day he is granted audience three times.

As an example of progress, this pictures a time when a powerful feudal lord rallies the other lords around the sovereign and pledges fealty and peace. The sovereign rewards him richly and invites him to a closer intimacy.
A twofold idea is set forth here. The actual effect of the progress emanates from a man who is in a dependent position and whom the others regard as their equal and are therefore willing to follow. This leader has enough clarity of vision not to abuse his great influence but to use it rather for the benefit of his ruler. His ruler in turn is free of all jealousy, showers presents on the great man, and invites him continually to his court. An enlightened ruler and an obedient servant — this is the condition on which great progress depends.

*The Image*

The sun rises over the earth:
The image of PROGRESS.
Thus the superior man himself
Brightens his bright virtue.

The light of the sun as it rises over the earth is by nature clear. The higher the sun rises, the more it emerges from the dark mists, spreading the pristine purity of its rays over an ever widening area. The real nature of man is likewise originally good, but it becomes clouded by contact with earthly things and therefore needs purification before it can shine forth in its native clarity.

LAST COW *caves in the barely discernible shadows..*
*Classes leave their marks to mingle with the germs and*
*fat and charcoal and ivory and enamel and lipstick*
*and chalk and magic gasses to attack the owe zone...*
*Just can't seem to help themselves.. tho they try hard*
*to understand — Make their lil marks and draw near*

Fig. 7-10. William Wiley, *A Suite of Daze* 1977
14 original etchings and haiku poem
17 x 13 x 1 1/2"
Courtesy of the Department of Special Collections,
University Library, University of California-Davis

is characteristic of Pop and Funk art in that it allows for a new perspective.

On the last page of the book which contains 16 etchings based on the I-Ching, Wiley wrote,

"...before the image plates I would throw the coins for the I-Ching, which has been a strong guide and source for me in many ventures sometimes able to reveal to me an attitude that's possible–available–regardless of the situations' positive or negative–I would consult the oracle then begin a plate attempting to keep in mind the attitude suggested by the text."

The return of the object in art presented new concerns; how to deal with the object in context of a realigned world view. Common objects were used in art that was named Pop, Funk, Assemblage, Happenings and Conceptual Art . While some works of Pop Art stand as records of the celebration of technology, and other works make social comment [25] , the main body of the art made use of objects from the material culture in the manner a Zen koan, the paradoxical statement used in Zen meditation, often including humor.[26] A typical example of a Koan is , what is the sound of one hand clapping, At midnight in Silla the sun is shining.

Much Funk and Pop Art is directly accessible when seen as a visual koan which allows for a new perspective. According to Oriental notions about the relationship between subject/object /artist/viewer, Pop art should be defined as presentation of paradox (objects taken out of context, repeated, changed in scale, or placed in illogical juxtaposition). The experience of the art allows potential for direct experience and new levels of awareness. The experience is essentially one of demystification and re-mystification transporting the viewer beyond thought or logic. Arneson, *Six-Pack*, (Fig.35) Rivers' *Webster and Cigars* of 1966 (Fig. 11) presents the viewer/participant with a paradox, a reference to an object, layered with references from other times, other places. Rivers' material, mixed-media collage on wood, appeals to the kinesthetic sense connecting by the sense of touch, sight, and by imagination and insight. There is no specified message or meaning intended, no logical conclusion. Rivers responded to the Zen/Tao notions as a "way of liberation," this world view gave the artist permission for the most personal expression, an American expression.

Attitudes about making art that germinated and took root in the 1950s and 1960s were concerned with redefining concepts such as reality, illusion, space, time, matter and spirit. Some of the art was called neo-Dada. Combined with some notions from the edges of European Dada and the popular notions from Zen, Tao, and the use of the *I-Ching*, William Wiley describes a "Zen-Dada" attitude saying that he sees Duchamp and American Dada as a "Zen way". [27]

After the mid-1950s a unique character of American art became evident. American art was now separated from its European precedents by a different philosophical base which included an assimilated and mutated

Fig. 11. Larry Rivers, *Webster and Cigars* 1966
Mixed media, collage on wood
13 1/4 x 16 x 13 1/4"
Private Collection

form of Far Eastern thought. Europe had assimilated Asian philosophy in its own manner while America linked itself to different aspects of Asian thought. Within this new hybridized American world view there is a collapse of the old hierarchy based on a European model; a new order of relationships result...relationships among man, nature and culture...art, science and politics. To restate Ibrahm Lassaw, "The Greco-Roman idealistic philosophy is one of static, eternal truths, perfection..a closed system. European tradition is now dying, its Platonic, Aristotelian and Roman bases have become ineffectual in the comprehension of the world today."

During the 1950s and 1960s artists were reading Existentialism, reconsiderations of Freud, Jung, and interpretations of Far Eastern philosophy. Artists who offered interpretations of the alternative view included: John Cage, Mark Tobey, Morris Graves, Minor White, Ad Reinhardt, Clifford Still, William Wiley, John Baldessari. They passed on Asian interpretations in their art and in their teaching. As Robert Arneson said, " It was around, everywhere! You had to be dead not to have been exposed to it." And John Baldessari said, " By the '50's Jung should be considered a popularizer of Eastern thought along with Alan Watts and John Cage."[28]

However, many art writers and critics completely ignoring the pervasive presence of Buddhist and Tao ideas, have assigned to Existentialism and Dada the total credit or blame for the motivation behind Pop and Funk Art.[29] Many artists, on the other hand, exploring the notions of existence, being and nothingness, spoke of existential thought as basically nihilistic, dualistic with a cynical, if not pessimistic, tone; they perceived Zen and Taoist writings as holistic, relativistic, paradoxical, humorous. They preferred the Zen "suchness" to nihilism. Some artists mixed conclusions from the two thought systems. They read Heidegger, Wittgenstein and Merleau-Ponty along with Herrigel, Watts, Suzuki and Jung. In typical American fashion many regarded these sources as "how- to" manuals or "parts lists" for a cultural revolution.

Buddhist (Zen) and Taoist thought, in interpreted form, were also disseminated throughout the country by the proliferation and cross fertilizations of the writings and activities of the Beat poets, Allen Ginsberg, Gary Snyder, Jack Kerouac, Phillip Whalen, Lew Welch, Diane DiPrima and Michael McClure[30] and writers like J.D. Salinger. By the 1960s many artists were sampling meditation practices, martial arts, and ikebana as well as travelling to Japan and China.

# Consequences in Art

The consequences of Asian influence in American art can be seen in two phases. First, there was an abandonment of Romantic European tendencies and the legacy of Abstract Surrealism, with its Freudian components.[31] In Surrealism the idea of metaphor had simply changed its form, for example, just as a lily represented the virgin in the Renaissance, a stylized fish represented Christianity in abstract surrealism. With the American Abstract Expressionists, once the artist discovers a personal gesture, metaphor dissolves and the work exists as "suchness." Process, product, subject, object are fused in existence and experience. The works of Pollock, Still, Reinhardt, Kline, Pousette-Dart, Guston, Onslow-Ford, Tobey, Graves and others are not meant to be "something" they simply "are." Many of the works were done in a meditative state and function as a centering device, or mandala, for the viewer.

The 1950s saw a continuation of artists' preoccupation with 'the void'; emptiness versus fullness. Attitudes about space were to be permanently changed. Knowledge of the void was gained through the meditative experience and the incorporation of Eastern practices into working methods (allowing things to happen, beginning with no plan). Some artists made mandalas, closely related to Japanese and Tibetan prototypes which serve as aids to meditation. They often referred to these works as mirrors or doorways. Zen and Tao discourse often appear in titles of paintings.[32]

The second phase was marked by the return of the object, the popular object at that, and the beginnings of "Performance Art" and the "Happening."[33]

Conceptions from Taoism and Zen were applied in new ways. For example, minimal abstraction can be likened, as Reinhardt noted, to the 8th Cowherding picture in Zen manuals, where one sees only the void. The return of the object is in like manner akin to the 10th cowherding picture, where the herdsman and cow reappear. (Now transformed, but one cannot see the transformation.) The objects used depend on such a transformation for their power.

Much of the paradox and humor used in Pop, Funk and Happenings, can be traced to Zen Buddhist and Taoist sources; for example the outrageous and irreverent behavior of the Taoist sage or the Zen master.[34] The use of humor in Zen and Tao writings is compatible with American humor. It is non-literary and points directly at the human condition without judgment, allowing for no taboos. The de-mystification of cultural sacred cows and the frank expressions of human sexuality went in tandem with a mystification of the common object expressing its mysterious and aesthetic potential as in Herinal (fig. 6). With collapsing dualities came the collapsing of hierarchies and judgments of all types. Distinctions between cultural divisions were dissolved. John Baldessari explained, "There was a leveling of previous conceptions of popular and high culture, hierarchies were abandoned."

The philosophical climate of the 1950s which shaped the character of the Oriental influence can be described as a rationalist / positivist or "scientific." Within this framework, the use of ideas and methods from Zen and Taoism were not considered religious or spiritual, they were considered instead to be ways of doing art and ways of being. They were seen as guides or instruction books showing the way to direct experience.

This a-religious, non-mystical, interpretation of Asian ideas was extracted from the most widely used Zen and Tao sources. Most publications stressed that these were not religious systems in the Western definition of the term. Religious or Romantic associations, along with academic or intellectual approaches, were not in vogue among non-conformist thinkers, writers and artists of the decade.[35]

The non-intellectual components of Taoist writings were compatible with American artists' nature; the rugged individual resembled the Taoist sage. There was little theorizing about the Far Eastern sources and practices. As Jane Teller phrased it, "They didn't talk about it, they just acted."[36] Some artists had already assimilated the Eastern world view into their own nature so that when it came around in a new form, it wasn't new to them.[37]

Since artists didn't talk about Zen or Asian sources in their work, critics didn't report it. This resulted in oversights and misinterpretations in much analytical and critical writing about the art. The catalytic effect of Far Eastern influence, for the most part, was missed, misunderstood or ignored.

An example of such misunderstandings can be found in interpretations of Jasper Johns' Target (Fig. 12) when the presence and impact of Far Eastern ideas on Johns and his contemporaries, and the influential text, "Zen and the Art of Archery," is ignored.[38] Target becomes a problem for a completely Western interpretation. When the Zen archer talks of a bow, a string and a

Fig. 12. Jasper Johns, *Target from the portfolio "For Meyer Shapiro"* 1973
Silkscreen
12 x 12"
Hofstra Museum Collection; Gift of Edwin Marks

target, his meaning is not that of a sportsman or a hunter. In the "Zen mind," the target is a mandala, a centering device, a place for facing paradox and of dissolving the duality between reality and illusion. Target is a place for transformation.

Each artist used the Eastern ideas and practices in a different way, but in general the Tao and Zen were described as " ways of liberation." They gave permission for direct experience and direct action. No formula, no model, no interpretation or explanation was required.[39] Assimilation of Oriental thought had far-reaching consequences. It functioned as a catalyst in an active solution of possibilities. The reasons for making art changed as well as working methods, attitudes toward materials, the notion of subjects and objects in art, the function of the work of art and the very self-image of the artist.

## Reasons for Making Art

Throughout the 1950s, reasons for making art were re-evaluated, and the creative process analyzed. The notions of tradition and desire were redefined. The Chinese critical term *chi* could be found in many artists' vocabularies and it was that life quality that was the ultimate measure of a work of art [40] Reasons for making art came from inside the artist.

No longer was art made as directed by totally Western traditions. No longer were works of art to have a direct relationship with objects in the sense that they were substitutions for appearances in the visible world. No narrative or didactic process was planned or implemented. No absolute meaning was to be determined. Instead, artists described preparations and procedures as 'yogic' or meditative and trusted in chance and spontaneity. Many artists also made use of humor or paradox in the manner of a Zen slap which the master would give to get the attention of the viewer.[41] Artists saw their works as the Zen Buddhist "direct pointing," as Suzuki and Watts related on many occasions, when the Zen master points at the moon, the student is warned not to mistake the finger for the moon.

Summary statements from a number of artists about the consequences of the assimilation of the Asian world view are so similar that they allow for some common conclusions.[42] First, will, desire and preconceived ideas or designs are unacceptable. Second, spontaneity and openness, coming from a transcended ego, allow for a connection with the spirit of nature and for the production of work that manifests that connection. Order is to be found, not imposed. Third, rationality/irrationality now have new meanings and a relativistic relationship; the rational is something to be surpassed not to be desired. The journey the artist undertook went beyond logic, beyond thought. Fourth, personal prefer-

ences, measure, value judgments are considered restrictions and inhibitions on the creative process.

When considering critical statements about Abstract Expressionism of the late 1940s and 1950s, and remembering the artists' notion that the reason for making art is self-discovery, one will re-read the texts with a new focus if the definition of "Self" is the Far Eastern one. The "Self" is defined as a transcendent state in which one experiences awareness of universal connections, awareness of wholeness. The "ego" is recognized as a temporary tool for living in the world of dualities and the purpose in art is to collapse dualities.[43]

In re-evaluating the reason for making art, the artist asks the Zen question, as Thomas Merton asked Ad Reinhardt, "Who is there to make the art?" [44] In art made from a Zen/Tao view, the ego must be surpassed or transcended. The conclusion is that personal expression is universal if art is made without superficial ego or self-conscious planning and that art, and the viewing of the art, is process. As Carolee Schneemann said, " Once you take in these ideas it changes your whole life, everything, even the way you tie your shoes. The reason for making art changes, and the way you make art changes." [45] Her trust in chance and randomness comes directly from the Tao and the I Ching. Schneemann's use of dust, the ultimate in chance operations (fig. 13,14), has been employed by a number of artists from Duchamp's *Dust Breeding Pictures*, to Wiley's bottle of dust in *Beatnik Meteor*, (fig. 74,75 ).

> The dust is used in this following spirit of the
> Tao:
> Existence, by nothing bred,
> Breeds everything.
> Parent of the universe,
> It smooths rough edges,
> Unties hard knots,
> Tempers the sharp sun,
> Lays blowing dust,
> Its image in the wellspring never fails.
> But how was it conceived - this image
> Of no other sire.
> *The Way of Life* according to Lao Tzu./Tr.
> Witter Bynner.

Schneemann allows things to happen in the spirit of the Tao. Happenings and performance have also been a significant body of Schneemann's work. They arise out of the trust in spontaneity and chance with no necessity of a preplanned order. The Happenings aim the viewer at a direct experience following the Zen method of direct pointing.

## Chants and Chance in the Working Method

Throughout the 1950s and 1960s the use of chants and chance in the preparation and practice of art as well as changed conceptions of space and matter are evident consequences of the catalytic effect of the assimi-

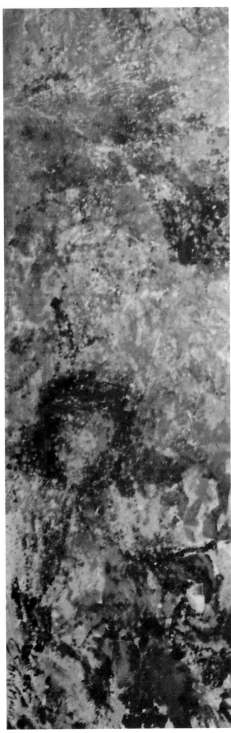

Fig. 13. Carolee Schneemann
*Scroll Painting with Exploded TV* (Dust Series),
1990
Ashes, ink, glass, printed fabric, computer board
on rag paper
52 x 211"
Collection of the Artist

Fig. 14. Carolee Schneemann
*Scroll Painting with Exploded TV*, 1990
(detail)

"Gravity is the root of grace, the mainstay of all speed"  —Lao Tzu

lation of a Far Eastern world view.[46]  Meditation and other ritual preparations were practiced in order to achieve a state in which the ego could be transcended, as Phillip Guston phrased it, "the work is done through me not by me."

From the 1940s into the 1960s many artists continued to practice various ways of yoga and other meditations, mantra chanting, and the use of I-Ching to promote trust in randomness and chance. Some explored the martial arts and ikebana.  The practices were passed on to the next generation, sometimes without a nod to their original sources. [47]

Also transmitted between generations was the notion that order, pattern or design could not be imposed but must be discovered.  This presupposed a passively-active state, allowing time for things to happen.  Forms were no longer placed upon a surface but were seen as emerging from the active void. The goal was direct experience which was to promote a kinesthetic, schematic contact with the viewer.  Baldessari tells of his colleagues being impressed by the underlying message of judo or karate,  because "the results were achieved not by brute force but by balance." [48]

Many artists found instructions on how to achieve balance and direct experience in several popular texts on Zen.  Many of the ideas contributed to changing the way they worked and their attitudes about the materials they used as in Rauschenberg's *Hound Track* (fig. 15). During much of the 1950s and 1960s  Herrigel's book "Zen and the Art of Archery"  was required reading in classes at the Art Institute of San Francisco, the Chicago Art Institute and at many universities and art schools. [49]

The book was extremely popular in ceramics classes where students learned  the idea of centering oneself as well as centering the clay.  It is instructive to think of the expression "self centered' from an Eastern world view.  In painting it promoted an identification with the tools and materials, a recognition of their contribution to the final work.  Herrigel's discussion about "becoming the bow, the string, the target,"  reappears in discourse used by artists.[50]

This new attitude toward materials and artists' working methods also appears in Performance art and the Happening.   Both of these art forms make use of  Zen and Tao concepts and practices. The Zen koan can be compared with the processes in both types of art experiences in the use of paradoxical juxtapositions, which foster direct experience, new perceptions and changed spatial orientations. A prototype of the Happening was done by Cage, Rauschenberg et al. at Black Mountain College, and in San Francisco the Beat poets, visual artists including Jess, Bruce Connor, and Jay DeFeo also staged  Happenings.[51]  The creative use of chance resulted from the artist maintaining an open, unprejudiced state, receptive to stimuli and silence, form and void equally, as in the state of Zen 'no-mind' or the Taoist "wu-wei" (doing - not doing).  In this state the artist, work and viewer become participants in a universal flow; the image or experience is relative to a set of continually changing relationships.

Working methods are no longer governed by traditional logic or rationality.  Meanings are sought beyond thought; the goal is direct experience or heightened awareness of connections within the universe.  Spontaneity,  a term  often heard in the 1950s and 1960s, is intended in its Eastern context as the "life force."  The Tao was defined as spontaniety or life force by many  writers and interpreters.  Within this world view dualities are not allowed, emptiness/fullness are complementary and a function of time and attention.

The following artists' statements explain various practices devised in an attempt to surpass the ego consciousness and to achieve a transcendent state.  In 1951 Jackson Pollock said, "I paint on the floor and that isn't unusual, the Orientals did that... It is only when I lose contact with the painting that the result is a mess..When I am in my painting I am not aware of what I'm doing." [52] Many artists practiced yoga or other types of meditation in preparation for beginning their work. Phillip Guston explained, "To get into this state, this other world demands extreme attention so that things can happen.  It's a state where you can catch it or miss it... I believe it was John Cage who once told me, 'when you start working everybody is in your studio, the past, your friends, enemies, the art world and above all, your own ideas, all are there.  But as you continue painting, they start leaving, one by one, you are left completely alone.  Then if you're lucky, even you leave." (quoted in D. Clarke)

Isamu Noguchi,  "I feel the more one loses oneself, the more one is oneself." (quoted in D. Clarke)

Morris Graves  " a painting is a way of knowledge....the act of painting is a meditation in itself. One must have in inner attitude of detachment." (quoted in D. Clarke)

Gordon Onslow-Ford,   "Painting in the Instant is an expression of unity, painting in the Instant happens with full attention while in a state of mind that corresponds to deep sleep." (personal interview with the author)

John Loftus  "In New York in the 1950s there wasn't a lot of talk,  artists just  went around behaving like Zen men, being open to possibilities." ( interview with the author)

Jane Teller "Ibram Lassaw introduced me to Zen in the '50s, he didn't tell me about it; by his working method, he demonstrated the pouring of molten metal and directed me to watch the Zen flow, it just happened." (personal interview with the author)

In 1953 Robert  Rauschenberg  made *Dirt Painting* for John Cage.  It  contained live plants, a continuous expression of spontaniety.  Ad Reinhardt adopted a personal formula in his own work as he understood it was done in the Oriental world.  Robert Arneson used the premise of detachment  and desirelessness in the manner in which he conducted his classes in ceramics at the University of California, Davis.  He instructed his stu-

Fig. 15. Robert Rauschenberg, *Hound (Tracks)* 1976
Tire Tracks in clay, silastic mold, dirt, resin binder, fiberglass, lead sheet
with epoxy soil patina
84 x 72 x 120"
Courtesy the Artist

dents to master the medium then guided them to give up ego attachment to "the perfect pot" by smashing it. Then, at one with the clay, the object is formed. Larry Rivers made a film "Pull My Daisy" with Jack Kerouac and Robert Frank in which there was no pre-planning; there was a trust in spontaneity and chance.

These practices and devices were explained in Zen and Tao sources and in interpretations of the I-Ching. Their use was spread by example and teaching, both formal and informal, through studio conversations and participation in poetry readings, concerts, and other events. The result was to cause the viewer to abandon the rational and leave behind prejudice and preconception. New ways of working had fostered new points of view and a new awareness of the relationship between art and life.

# Space: Form/Void
## (Tai Chi, Yin/Yang)

The notions of emptiness or fullness and Nothingness were popular topics from the late 1940s into the 1960s.[53] Most artists experienced a new awareness of the relationship between form and void. Hindu, Buddhist and Taoist notions of form and void were often discussed and compared with writings of Wittgenstein, Sartre, Heidegger and Merleau-Ponty.

After the 1950s the term "negative space" was not a viable one for art writers who wished to match their descriptions to artists' conceptions. In fact, the artists' attitude toward the void or the concept of emptiness can be one of the most accurate measures of Far Eastern influence. David Hockney explains that his awareness of new concepts of space (the active void) were first validated in writings on Eastern thought, and then through looking at Far Eastern art. He says that popular interpretations of modern physics, circulating in the 1970s, fascinated artists when those sources seemed to confirm what they had found earlier in the Zen/Tao texts. He says that the reason artists seek out sources is because they have confirmed their intuition.[54] Artists first read about ideas of relativity and chaos in Eastern mysticism and later compared the conceptions in popular explanations of modern physics especially, "The Tao of Physics."[55]

The compelling Oriental conceptions of form and void which attracted most artists can be found in an example of the writings from the *Tao Te Ching* which was also a text that was read and discussed in public and private artists' gatherings:

Thirty spokes will converge
In the hub of a wheel;
But the use of the cart
Will depend on the part
Of the hub that is void.

With a wall all around
A clay bowl is moulded;
But the use of the bowl

Will depend on the part
Of the bowl that is void.

R.B. Blakney *Tao Te'Ching*

Oriental conceptions of the void are of fullness, a ground of being out of which forms arise. Artists such as Rosenquist (fig.16), embrace the void and use it in art as a powerful positive force, a field of energy, which connects, gives rise to, and absorbs. It is not separate from matter, but part of its essence, a generating force. In the West, the Existential notion of the void, of being, of nothingness, was one to be feared, a modern version of the medieval purgatory, an abyss. The Existential ego struggles against nothingness and the fearful void.[56]Conceptions of space were altered by the incorporation and assimilation of the Far Eastern world view by most American artists during the 1950s and 1960s. And from this time this world view was passed on to each generation.

Form is void and void is form there is no separation, the void is a positive, generative field. Time is the mind of space and space is the body of time. Richard Pousette-Dart (conversation with the author)

When space, matter, was 'nothing' art was making something out of nothing. Now when space, matter, are 'something' art is making nothing out of something.
Ad Reinhardt (quoted in D. Clarke)

Forms appear out of consciousness. In western art the picture is generally conceived as seen in a frame or through a window. But the oriental image really exists only in our mind and heart and is thence projected or reflected onto space.
Morris Graves (quoted in D. Clarke)

Form and void are equal, one is no more important than the other, voids are fields of energy. Jane Teller ( interview with the author)

It was the notion of fullness versus emptiness as a notion of the void that drew me to Zen ideas and encouraged me to go further.
Harvey Himelfarb ( interview with the author)

One way I pass on these Eastern notions in my teaching is to insist that the students pay as much attention to the voids as to the forms, sometimes they are more important. And the humor, it changes ones perspective.
John Baldessari (interview with the author)

In Robert Barry's "invisible" pieces he insists that an active system is at work and present in the space. In the compositions of John Cage, he insists on the power and articulation of the spaces of silence. Given this new concept of space, the very existence of forms, objects and subjects of works of art were re-investigated. The very conception of matter began to interest artists in the 1950s.

# Subject/Object Relationship

In the 1950s the subject of the object of art becomes a condition, not a thing. Meanings are found in the verb, there is no separation of the subject and predicate.

> Pictures function as an aid to absorption. They cannot be judged by verisimilitude. [the work of art] ... is intended to convey an intelligible meaning and beyond, a condition of being, transcending even the images of thought, and only self -identification with the content of the work achieved by the spectator's own effort, can be regarded as perfect experience without distinction of 'religions' and aesthetic, logic and feeling. (Morris Graves paraphrasing Coomaraswamy.)

Throughout the 1940s and into the early 1950s many works of non-objective art made use of symbols. As mentioned earlier, artists followed their European mentors and borrowed a symbolic vocabulary from multiple sources within the history of image making. Everything was fair game, from African, Asian, Early Christian to Native American. Totemic forms, crosses, fish, lotus, populated the canvases and conjured associations with ages of elemental mystical connections. These works also contained Surreal or archetypal forms that functioned as personal metaphors. Eventually when each artist came to use his or her own personal gesture, divorced from any historic or symbolic association, the subject of his or her objects went beyond the symbolic, totemic or narrative, beyond metaphor.

On the other hand, Western critical interpretations continued to look for metaphor and described the personal gesture as a psychotherapeutic expression of ego or as scenic grounds for angst or anxiety. Sometimes the works were explained as expressions of rebellion or political protest. However, while these statements were made by the critics, artists proclaimed their apolitical nature.[57]

In keeping with the assimilated Asian world view the subject/object is the residue which creates a dynamic field of potential. "What is seen is what remains as evidence," said Phillip Guston. [58] In order to avoid the many misconceptions associated with art that related to the visible world, or the vocabulary of symbols, it seemed necessary for many artists to eliminate the object altogether. In fact Thomas Merton, in discussing the Far Eastern integration of form and void, once questioned his friend, Ad Reinhardt, about his use of the void, suggesting that perhaps Reinhardt was painting only the void.

The clue to the subject/object in the art of the 1950s abstractionists such as Ad Reinhardt, Clifford Still, Phillip Guston, Jackson Pollock, Gottlieb, Richard Pousette-Dart ( and many others) is in its function. They do not offer substitutes for objects in the visible world but are objects which act as mandalas, cosmic diagrams, in which the viewer can center herself/himself within the universe.[59]

The subject/object is transformation, awareness, existence or "being." Works can no longer be discussed by use of subject/predicate/modifier; there are no static, fixed meanings. The statement "reality is illusion" is not a paradox. As Alan Watts said, "What is the 'it' in 'it is raining?'"

An explanation for the subject of works in which objects from the visible world are used (Assemblage, Pop, Funk Art) can be found in the Zen story often repeated in publications of Suzuki, Watts and others. The story relates that before a Zen experience a mountain is a mountain, during the journey a mountain is no longer a mountain, after the experience a mountain is a mountain. The experience of the objects in much of Pop Art offers a pathway to a reconstituted awareness. A flag is a flag, a bottle is still a bottle, but it is in the juxtaposition and the experience that the potential for transformation lies. The frank presentation of sexual organs and other body parts was also done in the Zen sense, "no one thing more important than another." There was a de-mystification of sexuality and a reconsideration of the concept of beauty, as in Arneson's *Herinal* (Fig.6 ). Dualities between ugliness and beauty collapsed. In the process there was a mystification of the most common object.[60]

For example, the *Slant Step,* a mysterious object found by William Wiley and Bruce Nauman in 1965 (refer to illustrations by Robert Arneson, *Chinese Proverb* (fig. 37), and William T. Wiley, *The Slant Step* (fig. 4), has generated creative responses in art for over 20 years. The Slant Step, taken to Nauman's studio at the University of California, Davis, became the koan for a number of artists. Work was produced around this enigmatic object for which no one could find a use. Cynthia Charters writes, in an exhibition catalog for "The Slant Step Re-visited," held in 1984, "Regarding the Slant Step and Wiley's and Nauman's work of this period, both see the object as a "reinforcer." Nauman comments that the *Slant Step* was "problematic and useful" in his role . He recalls "...what I was trying to do was find a way to make objects...that appeared to have a function and... an excuse for the formal invention, but in fact, they didn't have any actual function and, in fact, the design of the pieces was arbitrary or invented. *The Slant Step* was such an example of that because it was something that everybody thought had a function until you really tried to use it."

The use of the Slant Step as the use of the koan is an interior journey, the paradox serves as the initial map, just as the Slant Step pointed the way yet was not the answer; the map is not the territory. In Zen, the traveller is directed to find his own nature, the nature of his environment and to "be" in harmony. Sucessful practice of Zen does not allow a distinction between the individual and his environment, for ultimately they are one. The western aphorism "to thine own self be true" has a different meaning for the Zen artist who is one with his environment both natural and cultural. The Self is a radically transformed and expanded entity.

Fig. 16. James Rosenquist, *Somewhere to Light from the portfolio New York International* 1966
Silkscreen
17 x 22 1/2"
Hofstra Museum; Gift of Dr. Milton Gardner

Therefore, if an artist is American, the Zen artist is truly American, to the core. The work will not look Oriental, it will look American. The work can only be described as individualistic in the original meaning of that term, undivided, not separated from the whole. (The Western meaning of individual is actually " dividual," divided or separated from others.) For example, Marisol uses her own face in many of her works, see *Fishing* (Fig.20). Critics called the practice narcissism. "I'm always there (in my studio) when I'm working. I work very often at night. I can't call up a friend at one in the morning to make a cast of his face. But when I make a cast of my own face I file it down or alter it by sandpapering. Whatever the artist makes is always a self portrait. Even if he paints a picture of an apple or makes an abstraction. When I do a well-known person like John Wayne, I'm really doing myself" (from Marisol, Catalogue of an Exhibition, Worcester Art Museum, Mass., 1971). Marisol's statement was followed by Richard Stuart Teitz' analysis, "Her aloneness at the moment is exaggerated in a provocative manner."

Aloneness, self, nothingness are words with very different meanings within the Occidental and Oriental worlds. The Orient defines self or individual in the original sense of the word at its origin as un-divided from the whole, but a unique expression of it. In keeping with Marisol's expressed interest in Buddhist and Taoist ideas her work should be viewed instead as an expression of the realization of connection between all beings and things. No one is alone if all things are connected. Another alternative expression in keeping with a holistic world view is that "nothing" means no one thing; one thing is all things.

A sound man's heart is not shut within itself
But is open to other people's hearts:
I find good people good
And I find bad people good
If I am good enough;
I trust men of their word,
And I trust liars
If I am true enough;
I feel the heart-beats of others
Above my own
If I am enough of a father,
Enough of a son.
*The Way of Life* According to Lao Tzu
Witter Bynner

At a faculty lecture (Spring 1989), Robert Arneson described his use of his own face by saying that "it is really not me, not the ego me."

Like Baldessari, Arneson, and Wiley, Marisol's work is permeated with wit and humor. Its straightforward directness, pointing at the human condition, allows the viewer a new perspective, new awareness. It is the caricature or comic quality without literary or symbolic reference that is the link between American humor and Zen humor and which distinguishes it from humor in the European tradition.

The concept of *yin-yang* is also operative in the new subject/object relationship. Pondering *yin-yang* leads to a reconsideration of the relationship between matter and spirit or essential nature. Matter is seen as the visible carrier of the spirit. Matter is conceived of in an Einsteinian relativistic state. Therefore, the subject of the object of the work of art is essence or 'ness..the life quality, the Chinese *chi*. Within a world view made up of assimilated Far Eastern conceptions subject, object, and working method become "spontaniety." And when common objects are used by an American artist the result is American art; The more American, the more Zen/Tao.

The direct and indirect effect of the presence of Asian thought in American culture, and especially in the art world, can be examined by considering the attitudes, life and work of several American artists. It must be emphasized, however, that in this study these few stand for the many; their reactions are typical of American artists during this period.[61]

# Conclusion

Perhaps there is no better way to comprehend the problems with a totally Occidental interpretation of American art of the 1950s and 1960s than to engage in a dialogue with a specimen text. I do not mean to single out the author of the following statements but, in the spirit of randomness, his statement came to my attention at an auspicious time. It is intended to stand for the common attitudes and judgments that have been made over the years about Pop and Funk art. And it is intended to point to the result of the neglect of the Asian influence in interpretations of the art and culture of that time. I will interrupt the text to demonstrate the alternative attitude. The statements come from *The Joys and Sorrows of Recent American Art*, Allen S. Wellei, Chicago, 1968.[62]

> A combination of several characteristics of the contemporary mood in art—its preoccupation with the machine, with words and letters, with techniques and materials developed for mass production, with anonymity—makes understandable, even inevitable, the appearance of Pop Art.

In the West the the word "anonymity" involves the ego, the name of the artist, and refers to the "creator of the work" as if the work and the artist were not connected. As in the West, the concept of God is separate from that of humankind. Taken in the Asian sense, the term could not even actually exist in the realm of art, but if used, it suggests the (re)placement of the ego, integrated or submerged in the dynamics of the work; the work and the artist are connected above the level of ego. As an example, if Rauschenberg, Wiley, or Arneson use a Coke bottle in their work, they trust that if the work is done in a state where they are connected to universal consciousness, the work will speak of them because it is their unique expression of the universal. It does not have, or require, an ego identity. Is it not the case, for instance, that the viewer is able to identify the work, even if not signed, as a Wiley, a Rauschenberg, an Arneson, etc.? Is the work truly anonymous? Their works of art are the carrier of their identity fused or connected to the identity of the viewer; matter informed by the spirit. Even when the artist uses his / her own face, be it reproduced in multiples or placed out of context, in the Asian world view it does not have an attachment to the ego, but in the Tao sense is "the outward container" of the spirit, and is just as valid, no less, no more, than the Coke bottle. The work does not point to the artist or the subject but points the viewer to his/her own experience, yet resonates from the unique consciousness that is the artist.

> This movement [Pop Art] reached its height when Robert Rauschenberg received the top prize at the 1964 Venice Biennale but seems to have quickly subsided. No movement in recent times emerged so swiftly, excited so much comment in quarters that are not ordinarily concerned with art, and wore out its welcome so soon.

The idea that there are movements that begin and end is another example of Western dualistic or linear thinking with separable beginnings, middles and ends. Instead when conditions are seen as existing within a dynamic relationship, the ideas that crystallized in Pop and Funk art can be likened to the genetic material on the DNA molecule. The material is always present in every new offsping even though sometimes not manifest in visible features. Pop Art grows out of what came before, and could not have been, without abstract expressionism and the art that preceded it. When one considers the issue from the point of the Asian world view, after abstract expressionism and its new conception of the void as the generative energy field, when the object returns, it is within that field and its existence is a set of conditional relationships.

> Pop art represented a new realism, in which art becomes an object like any other object in the material world, in which the banalities of everyday life are accepted completely and uncritically.

In an Asian interpretation, the subject in Pop and Funk art has nothing to do with the "object," the object is not a metaphor but exists in conditional relationship with the viewer/participant (refer to Rosenquist's statement in artists' section). The subject of the object is existence, experience, potential. There is a Zen saying that when something is boring for two minutes, try it for four and so on, until it becomes interesting–"banalities of everyday life..." (The reader is asked to review Baldessari's and Rauschenberg's statements in the individual biographies.) The artists who function from an assimilated Asian world view cannot conceive of anything as being banal. As Gary Snyder says, "One of the results of a Zen attitude is a de-centering of the sacred." As John Cage says, "Life is an ocean of possibilities."

"accepted completely and uncritically..."

In the West, a work is matched against some outside criterion. Criticism is leveled at the ego; right and wrong comes from someone else's judgment. In the Asian world view, measure or judgment is always relative to context. The ultimate measure is the balance and harmony of the universe or the *chi*. The recognition of the balance can only come from within. Acceptance is in the Taoist sense of receptivity, acknowledgment and awareness, not in the Western sense of tolerance or critical acclaim.

> Pop art suggests the swift obsolescence of ideas that is characteristic of the world of commerce, the use of ephemeral materials, indifference to permanence.

"indifference to permanence"

The Buddhist notion of impermanence or transience, flux or the continuum, is one of the concepts that intrigued the artists when those notions first circulated (refer to J.D. Salinger's discussion in the text). The acknowledgment of "non-attachment" was a liberating force. The ephemeral was a condition that generated countless works of art, and continues to do so. It is a celebration and acknowledgment of impermanence. (A text that was highly influential on this subject was Alan Watts' *The Wisdom of Insecurity*.) A re-aligned attitude toward attachments and permanence (an idea

of relativity) arose during a time when Zen and Tao sources were pervasive. The conception was reaffirmed in the 1970s when the popular writings on modern physics likened these Asian ideas to the new conceptions of space, time and the existence of matter. (*The Tao of Physics*)

> Pop art accepts the visual assault we have experienced from advertising, comics, television, packaging. It is indifferent to craftsmanship and avoids the personal touch.

The artists in this exhibition, who are only a few, are meant to stand in for American artists on the mainstream who came of age in the 1950s and 1960s. In this era artists consider the experience of this art not as a "visual assault" but to be a visual feast. That "permission to be American" of which Baldessari speaks, was granted by the assimilation of the Asian world view, and the "leveling," about which Arneson, Baldessari and Wiley speak, gave the comic and the cartoon its place as an expression of the essence or *chi* of American culture. The items listed by the writer can be described as an assault only if one holds to the view of "high art"–"low art", the Western idea of linear progress and hierarchical structure, the expectation that art should do some specific thing and be about certain subjects. The aforementioned view is precisely the view that collapsed with the assimilation of the Asian ideas in the 1950s and 1960s.

> It (Pop Art) does not create symbols, and it is not satire. It is in a sense a protest against all forms of earlier art, but it is not in itself a comment on life.

The works can best be described by the Zen term "suchness"; indeed, they are not a symbol or a protest. The earlier forms of art are all present on that DNA molecule, but not all are manifest at the same time. The humor is not satire but Zen humor; direct pointing to the elemental human condition, not literary based, not political. There is no absolute meaning to each work but, like the Zen koan, it presents the participant with a paradox which allows the potential for transformation. It is not a comment on life. It "is." To repeat Alan Watts, one would ask the Western interpreter of this American art, "What is the "it" in, 'it is raining'?"

# Notes

1 Taisen Deshimaru, *Questions to a Zen Master*, Dutton 1985

2 Research to date for unpublished text, Geri DePaoli, "The Great Waves : The Impact and Consequences of Asian Thought on American Culture, Post WW II", includes over 125 interviews, written correspondence, and archival data which provides testimony about a profound awareness and use of Asian art and ideas in the lives and art of the artists. Also showing the effect of the influence of East Asian thought on American Artists see: Gail Gelburg, Far Eastern Philosophical Influences on Environmental Art: 1967-1987, Dissertation, CUNY 1988, David J. Clarke, The Influence of Oriental Thought on Postwar American Painting and Sculpture, Garland NY 1988.

3 For a comprehensive treatment of the subject see: Rick Fields, *How the Swans Came to the Lake: A History of Buddhism in America*. Shambala, 1981; Robert S. Ellwood Jr., *Alternative Altars: Unconventional and Eastern Spirituality in America*, University of Chicago Press, 1979. also see: Diane Apostolos-Capadonna ed, *Art Creativity and the Sacred*, Crossroad, NY 1984; Maurice Tuchman et al, *The Spiritual in Art: Abstract Painting 1890-1985*, Abbeville NY 1986, and D.J. Clarke, G. Gelburd dissertations. For more information see writings about the Theosophical societies in America and their impact on art and culture in the early century.

4 In a personal interview with the author, Gary Snyder commented on the influence of Asian thought on American poetry and recommended these additional references: Beongheon Yu, *The Great Circle: American Writers and the Orient*, Wayne State University Press 1983, and R. Ellwood.

5 R. Fields, R. Ellwood.

6 R. Fields, R. Ellwood, B. Yu.

7 Perhaps the ideas worked in true Taoist fashion as expressed in the Tao Te Ch'ing which describes the best leader as one who guides and advises and in the end, "lets them believe that they did it themselves." There are many other possibilities for the neglect of the consideration of Asian influence on American art; some of which are specific to each individual and some to the political and philosophical environment under which the critics wrote. The reasons given range from a fear of insufficient knowledge of the Asian philosophy itself to a prejudice based on a Western European chauvinism. In my interviews with over 125 artists to date the great majority say that, even though Asian thought has been a profound influence, writers and critics do not ask about it and when the artist volunteers the information it is dismissed or ignored.

8 Thomas S. Kuhn *The Essential Tension: Selected Studies in Scientific Tradition and Change*, University of Chicago 1977. For further discussion of the effect of a change in world view on the life and work of an artist see: David Blinder, "The Controversy over Conventionalism", The Journal of Aesthetics and Art Criticism XLI/3 Spring 1983.

9 Interview with the author.

10 M. Tuchman et al. The Spiritual in Art.

11 Terminology used in discussing art made with a holistic world view poses the same problems as those faced in modern physics because it is the nature of language to separate. (i.e. in physics the term space/time is now used instead of space and time). In art form and void, subject and object now have different references. And it is in part due to this linguistic problem that the art of the 20th century has been difficult to analyze and discuss. The term viewer/participant must be used because in this realm there cannot be an objective viewer. The observer changes what is observed.

12 Robert Janes, Professor Emeritus, University of Maryland coined the phrase "sin and science" in a personal interview with the author about his writings in sociology and the mechanism of influence on a culture.

13 For further information about sources which acted as vehicles for the transmission of Asian ideas to American culture see: R. Fields; G. Gelburd; D. Clarke; and for specific models for the manner in which the influence functioned see: Gerald Rosen, *Zen in the Art of J.D. Salinger*, Creative Arts Book, Co. Berkely Ca. 1977; Chicago Review, Summer 1958; copies of IT IS magazine 1968.

14 G. Gelburd, D. Clarke. These ideas also recur in over 90 of my interviews with artists to date.

15 Taisen Deshimaru, *Questions to a Zen Master*; Charles Tart, *Transpersonal Psychologies* and writings in the *Journals of the Institute for Noetic Sciences*.

16 Schwarz, *The Matrix of Modernism*, and Karlfried Graf Durkheim, Zen and Us, tr 1987, Dutton, NY 1987

17 Artists read Nietzsche, Sartre, Kierkegaard, and Wittgenstein and compared them to the writings on Buddhism, especially regarding the concept of emptiness and the ego. Evidence of this comes from the archives of the University of California, Davis: Letters to Gary Snyder from Kerouac, Whalen, Kyger, DiPrima specifically, and an interview with John Cage.

18 The civil rights movement contains many ideas of Ghandi; the Zen and Tao material was also present and mixed with what was conceived to be a return to the original principles of Christianity.

19 Beginning in the '50s the "yin-yang" concept, the complementary nature of what had been previously defined as opposites, became part of the American vocabulary.

20 For further information and bibliography see Tuchman, "The Spiritual In Art", the writings of Clement Greenberg and his insistence on a solely formalist interpretation of the art. A perception of a formalist critical attitude which shunned spiritual or mystical content in the 50's and 60's was described to me in conversations with Richard Pousette-Dart, Robert Motherwell, David Hockeny, Kenneth Tyler. (extensive material to be included in text (unpublished) "The Great Waves: The Impact and Consequences of Asian Thought on Post WW II American Culture, by G. DePaoli.

21 K.G. Durckheim, pp11-12.

22 Material from a personal interview with John Loftus, Department of Art, Hobart and William Smith Colleges. Also see: Emil deAntonio, *Painters Painting*. In this way of thinking the subject and object are fused, the work of art is not a metaphor or a symbol but exists a "suchness" (the Zen conception of being). The intent of the artist is to direct the viewer/participant to direct experience.

23 Gerald Rosen, *Zen and the Art of J.D. Salinger*.

24 The Self with the upper case "S" refers to the True Self as represented in the Ten Oxherding pictures used to teach Zen. (the ox represents the True Self and the seeker pursues the ox.) see D.T. Suzuki, Essays in Zen Buddhism for complete discussion. It is a state beyond ego and beyond dualities wherein one realizes a connection to the whole. Gordon Onslow-Ford has written about this state referring to it as "Mind", and he stresses the importance of this transformation in a true artists work. personal interview with the author.

25 For a comprehensive review and critical re-interpretation of American Art of the '50s and 60's which continues to neglect the impact and consequences of Asian notions on the artists intent, process, product and meaning see catalog for the exhibition, *Made*

in the USA, University Art Musuem, Berkeley, 1987. Also see: Lucy Lippard, *Pop Art*, NY 1988 and Carol Anne Mashun, *Pop Art and the Critics*, UMI Press 1987. These laudable efforts do indeed apply many previously neglected points of view to the re-interpretation of the art, but again without the Asian element, without the recognition of an altered world view of the artists, the analyses are incomplete and often needlessly apologetic and complex.

26 Koans were known and discussed commonly by the Beat writers, musicians and the visual artists in the avant garde centers in San Francisco, Chicago and New York in the '50s and '60s. Koan was often described by Alan Watts, D.T. Suzuki, E. Herrigel and other writers as a Zen device which confronts the viewer with a paradox, a non-rational statement ( i.e. What is the sound of one hand clapping?). The consideration of the statement denies the inevitability of a logical answer, provides a space for transformation and leads the ponderer beyond thought. Compare the ideas of Carol Mashun in Pop Art and the Critics in relation to the concept of transformation.

27 For further reading on the connections of Dada, DuChamp and Asian thought see comments and bibliography in Tuchman, *The Spiritual in Art*, and Linda Henderson, *The Fourth Dimension and Non-Euclidian Geometry in Modern Art*, Princeton, 1983. D. Clarke, G. Gelburd. The influence of the alternative Asian world view pre-dates the 50's in Europe and America and this early exposure and the consequences of it needs a great deal of study.

28 Personal interview with the author.

29 A review of the writings on Pop art from early writings by Alloway to the recent publication by Mashun shows the attempt to explain and analyze the art by the application of Western philosophical sources and systems of measure. In most cases this results in a complex argument which leaves the residue of an apology. A survey of the discussions in The Dictionary of Literary Biography, in the volumes on Beat Literature, one finds a similar situation. In those essays in which the Buddhist element in Beat culture is not mentioned one can clearly see the problem. If one truly looks at Beat literature and traces its sources, the philosophical references are to Buddhism or the Tao and not to Dionysus. Perhaps historians and critics still look to the Greeks but the artists did not. Just as many art historians and critics use Freud to interpret work of artists who are reading Jung.

30 For further reference on the history of the Beat era see: Thomas Albright, *Art in the San Francisco Bay Area*, Berkeley, 1985. Much information about the spread of Zen ideas in the 50's and 60's was provided by Gary Snyder and can be documented in the material in the archives of Gary Snyder at the University of California, Davis, department of Special Collections.

31 See catalog of exhibition: *The Interpretive Link: Abstract Surrealism to Abstract Expressionism*, Whitney Museum of Art, 1986.

32 Referring to the use of terms in artists' conversation and in titles of paintings Dore Ashton in The New York School: A Cultural Reckoning, NY 1971, speaks of , "John Cage's Zen rhetoric" showing up among the artists. It is one aim of this study to demonstrate that the use of Zen terms and the legacy of the assimilation of the world view goes much beyond what can be described as "rhetoric".

33 The events that were defined as "Happenings" at Black Mountain College and in clubs and in the streets of SanFrancisco in the 50's were inspired by ideas and practices encountered in Zen and Tao material and the I-Ching. The material was available in many popular publications and transmitted by interpreters such as: John Cage, Jack Kerouac, Gary Snyder, Alan Ginsberg, Ad Reinhardt, Clifford Still to name but a few. See: Albright, Ashton, and Richard Kostelanetz, John Cage, London, 1971.

34 The notion of the artist modelling after the rugged, natural, outdoor life might even be considered to have contributed to the change in domestic interiors and fashion in clothing with the interest in natural fibers, jeans, and the general increase in pluralism of style and informality in dress.

35 The sources of information about Zen, Taoism, the I-Ching (ideas and practices) which were available and used by artists did not describe Zen or Tao ideas as a religion in the manner of the western understanding of that term. The concepts were often described as a "way of liberation". If anything , the ideas were compared to psychoanalysis or modern physics.

36 From an interview with Jane Teller about her experiences as a member of the Sculptor's Guild in New York City in the 1940's and 50's. In interviews with John Baldessari, John Loftus, Roland Peterson, William T. Wiley, Richard Pousette-Dart, Dorothy Dehner, Jane Teller and David Hockney , all of the artists insisted that the Asian material led them to seek direct experience, with their materials, with their art and to turn inward for 'the answers'. All of them said that they did not consider the Zen and Tao sources to be either a new abstract philosophy or a substitute for any Western religion, but a practical matter, a way to be and do art.

37 See writings on Jackson Pollock's early years and his association with Krishnamurti, Francis O'Connor. and Maurice Tuchman, *The Spiritual in Art.*

38 see discussions of Johns' Target and the painting "Tantric Detail", in Mark Rosenthal, *Jasper Johns: Work since 1974*, Philadelphia Museum of Art 1989. Note the avoidance of any reference to the impact and consequences of a lifelong interest in Asian philosophy and his insistence upon finding sources in Western Art.

39 Zen, Tao and the Vedanta were called "ways of liberation", by Alan Watts and Joseph Campbell on numerous occasions in their very popular texts.

40 See Johns' statements about breath in Mark Rosenthal, and references to artists' attitude about breath in David Clarke, and Gail Gelburd.

41 The "and" between meditation and humor actually dissolves as it does in time/space. Both processes (meditation and humor) allow one to achieve a new perspective, awareness of relativistic relationships, leads to insight which allows the perception of duality to collapse.

42 My own research includes archival data on over 100 artists and pesonal interviews with 90 artists including: John Cage, Gordon Onslow-Ford, Richard Pousette-Dart, Robert Motherwell, Dorothy Dehner, Aaron Siskind, Jane Teller, Robert Arneson, William T. Wiley, Wayne Theibaud, Harvey Himelfarb, Cornelia Shulz, Carolee Schneemann, John Baldessari , Eric Fischl, Phillip Pearlstein , David Hockney, Wayne Miller , Roger Shimomura, Naoto Natagawa, Alastair Noble all of whose ideas have contributed to this publication . For additional data see material in: David Clarke, Gail Gelburd.

43 See discussion of the ego and the artist by Francis O'Connor, "The Psychodynamics of Creativity", in The Art Journal of the College Art Association, Fall 1988, -and many additional writings covering the subject by O'Connor in the Psychoanalytic Press, Dr. O'Connor has provided invaluable sources and ideas during the course of this research.

44 Quoted from Philip Guston correspondence to David Clarke.

45 Personal interview with Carolee Schneemann.

46 The practice of meditation, the use of the I-Ching and the study of the Martial Arts were common during the 50's and 60's in the major art centers as well as in various urban areas across the country. Experimentation and discussion was pervasive.

47 Very few critical or art historical sources even acknowledge the presence of Asian materials in the artists environment, and when they do they dismiss them as unimportant, either directly or by neglect. This neglect has resulted in some flawed analyses or complete misunderstanding. i.e. in Judith Goldman, *James Rosenquist*, NY 1985, p. 35, Rosenquist says, " I wanted the space to be more important than the imagery. I wanted to use images as tools. But it just didn't happen, because the dumb critics said, " Oh look, I can recognize that, that's a car, that's a hot dog, that's popular." My work didn't have anything to do with popular images like chewing gum."

48 Personal interview with the author

49 Data from personal interviews, archival research, i.e. personal interview with Harvey Himelfarb, University of California, Davis. "It was used as a text. I have given away over 500 copies. I tell my photography students to substitute photography for archery and they will understand."

50 i.e. Pollock's statement about "becoming the painting", in his teaching Arneson refers to the text when he speaks about centering the clay.

51 See discussion about the chronology of Happenings in T. Albright, *Art in the SanFrancisco Bay Area*, and R. Kostelanetz, John Cage.

52 B. H. Friedman, *Energy Made Visible*, London, 1972, Pollocks working method is described as "pure Yoga.

53 Schwarz, *Matrix of Modernism*, p.17.

54 Personal interview with the author.

55 Other sources on connections between modern physics and mysticism which were provided in interviews with artists: David Bohm, *Wholeness and the Implicate Order*, Gary Zukov, T*he Dancing Wu Li Masters*, NY: 1979, Fritjof Capra,*The Tao of Physics, NY: 1976.*

56 Existentialism appeared at first to match Zen notions of nothingness or emptiness but on further consideration artists perceived a nihilistic and dualistic quality. This process was discussed and references given in an interview with John Cage by the author.

57 The sequence of events relating to the political nature of the art community is well recorded in D. Ashton, *The New York School.* There is much artist testimony of mis-interpretation of their motives and work and of the fact that they were never asked about Oriental sources in their work. For example, in a personal interview with John Baldessari, when asked why his interest and use of Asian ideas has never been recorded he replied that, "no one ever asked".

58 Phillip Guston statement to David Clarke, he had much to say about the influence of Suzuki and Asian thought.

59 The holistic world view shared by artists can be clearly extracted from material in D.Clarke, G. Gelburd and from interviews by the author for The Great Waves (unpublished text)

60 John Cage said in a personal interview that these ideas about Buddhist 'nothingness' are also in the writings of Wittgenstein and that he shares bibliography with Johns and Rauschenberg. A book that Cage referenced was F.J. Streng, *Emptiness: A Study in Religious Meaning*, Nashville 1967, he referred to the section comparing the notion of emptiness in Buddhist thought in the writings of Nagarjuna and in the writings of Wittgenstein.

61 Artists such as; Semour Locks, Jess, Jay DeFeo, Bruce Connor, Robert Hudson, Wallace Berman, Andy Warhol, Roy Lichtenstein, Eva Hesse, are only a few critical artists of the 50's whose works should be explored in light of the impact and consequences of their exposure and use of Zen/Tao, I-Ching and other Asian ideas and practices. Information on 125 artists is included in *The Great Waves.*

62 See C. Mashun, *Pop Art and the Critics*, L. Lippard, *Pop Art*, and other more recent writings on the subject. Some add other methodology including semiotics, Feminism, and Marxism but all repeat the early interpretations and do not address the presence, impact and consequences of the volume of information and experience with Asian thought and practice which was part of each artist's life.

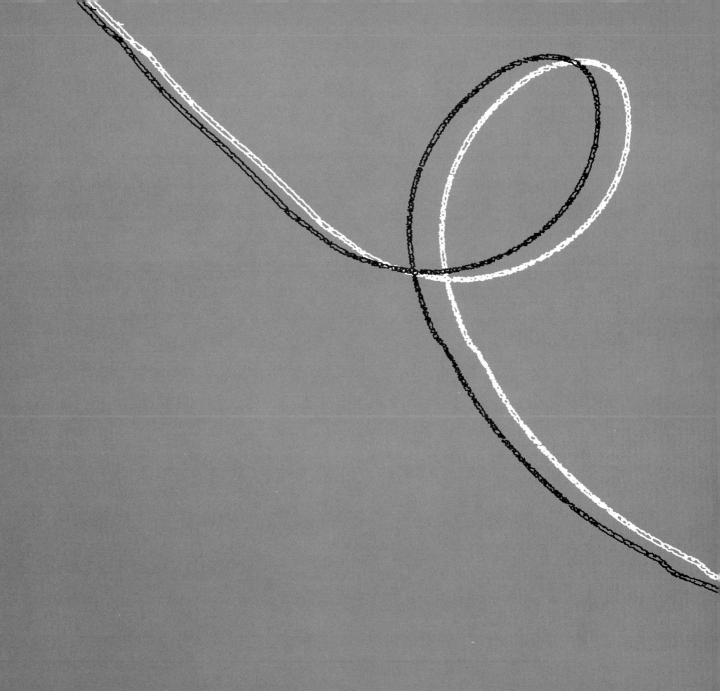

Fig. 17 Robert Arneson
*Trophy All American* 1964
Ceramic sculpture
26 x 12 x 7"
Jedermann Collection, N. A.

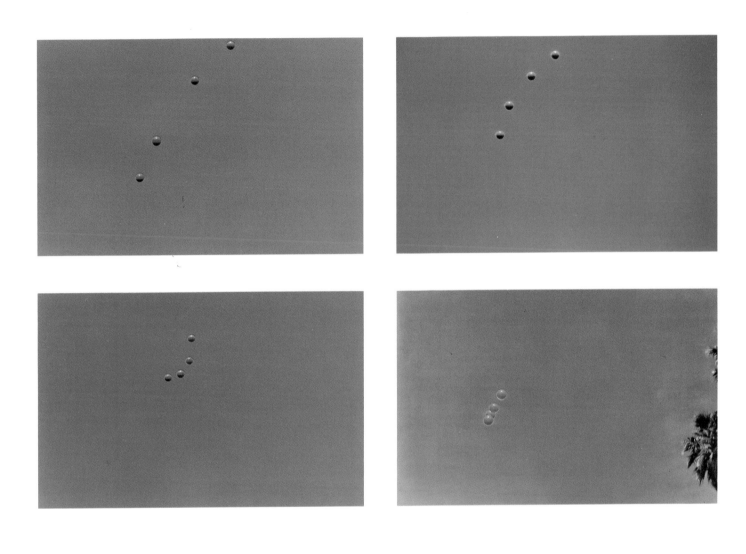

Fig.18 John Baldessari
*Throwing Balls into the Air to Get a Straight Line*
(Best of 4 of 36 tries)  1972-73
4 color photographs
13 1/4 x 20"
Collection of Dr. and Mrs. Paul Vanek, Toronto, Canada

Fig.19 Patricia Johanson
*Leonhardt Lagoon,* Dallas Texas

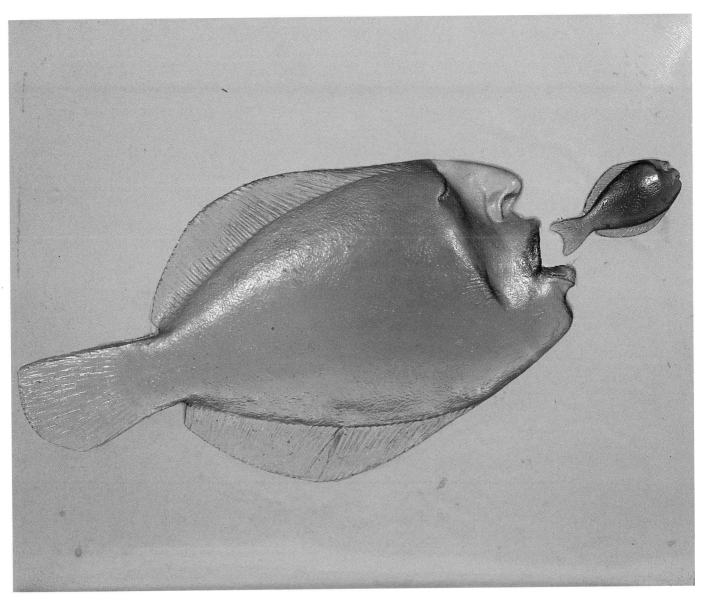

Fig.20 Marisol
Fishing c. 1970
Cast acrylic
14 1/2 x 16 5/8"
Hofstra Museum Collection; Gift of Dr. and Mrs. Joseph Tucker

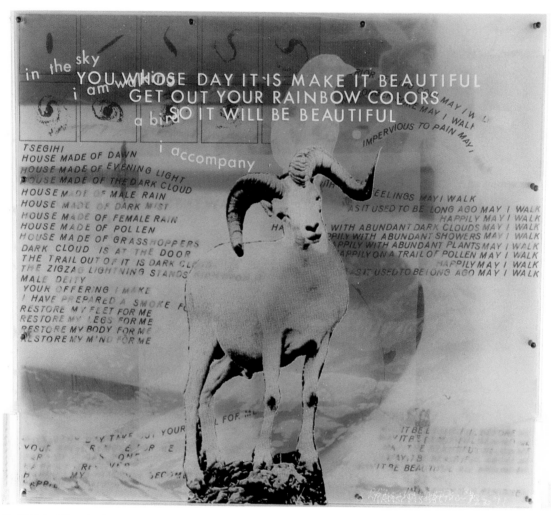

Fig. 21 Robert Rauschenberg
*Opal Gospel* 1971
Silkscreen on 9 acrylic panels
18 x 20" ea.
Hofstra Museum Collection; Gift of Carole and Alex Rosenberg

Fig. 22 Michelle Stuart
*Sabi 1* 1989
Encaustic, pigments, plants and shale on linen-backed rag paper
mounted on canvas
77 x 77"
Courtesy Fawbush Gallery

Fig.23 Christopher Wilmarth
*When Winter on Forgotten Woods* 1979/80
Bronze and glass
18 x 12 x 6"
Private Collection

# Pointing to:
# the Center of Experience

## by Gail Enid Gelburd

The world seems to explode in a myriad of directions and we feel compelled to search for a centripetal force which will pull it back together. We proceed on a quest for that one element that is suspended in a void, bombarded by opposing forces, absorbing them all while remaining stable. Life, art, culture, and society have seemed disparate and fragmented since the mid-1960s. The art has been called "Pluralist" as we are propelled through movements called Minimalism, Conceptualism, Realism, Environmentalism, Performance, Process, Post-Modernism, Neo-Geo, Graffiti, and Neo-Expressionism. Andy Warhol said that each of us would be famous for fifteen minutes — yet our art movements seem to prevail for only five. Is there a point where they meet, a thread that runs through, tying together the art of this era? A close look at the art of this seemingly Pluralist age reveals a thread that, while transparent, is the veil that cloaks the forms. The history and politics of the time reveals a transparent thread which is a part of the very fabric of our society. This thread is woven by the torrent of contact the United States has had with Japan, China, Vietnam, Cambodia, Laos, and Sri Lanka, and with the philosophies of those nations: Buddhism, Taoism, and Zen.

In the late 1960s American contact with East Asia was occurring in politics, economics, music, poetry, and art. In the late 1960s over 11,000 Hong Kong Chinese emigrated to the United States. The U.S. ratified an agreement with other nations to charter the Asian Development Bank; the Montreal World's Fair held a Kabuki performance; and Maharishi Mahesh Yogi became a spiritual leader. Bruce Lee starred in movies showing old-fashioned values of good versus evil in a distinctly Oriental (Kung-fu) way for correcting the ills of society. Sri Chinmoy gave a concert at the Indian Cultural Center in New York, and the Beatles' Sergeant Pepper album was filled with Indian instrumentation. A concert for Bangladesh, to help those suffering after the secession from Pakistan, featured Indian music by Ravi Shankar. The 1972 Winter Olympics were held in Sapporo, Japan. During the period beginning in 1965, several exhibitions of Oriental art appeared at major museums; "Yomato-e" at the Los Angeles County Museum, "Ancient Sculpture from India" at the Metropolitan Museum of Art, New York, and the "Singer Collection of Chinese Objects" at the Asia House in New York. In 1970, there were six major exhibitions of Oriental art including the John D. Rockefeller Oriental Collections at the Asia Society Galleries and "Traditions of Japanese Art" at the Fogg Art Museum of Harvard University. The Metropolitan Museum of Art held an exhibition of Chinese calligraphy as well as an exhibit titled "Beyond the Great Wall of China" in 1973, and in 1974, "New Visions of Classical China" was shown at the National Gallery in Washington, D.C.

In the 1970s, the United States was fighting in Laos, yet at the same time lifted restrictions on travel to China, removed a twenty-one year embargo on trade with China, and voted to give the People's Republic of China a seat on the United Nations Security Council. The Tibetan Dalai Lama went on a ten nation tour to show Buddhism to the Western World in 1974. In 1975, the Korean religious leader, Sun Myung Moon, organized the Unification Church. There were an estimated 400,000 Asians in New York City by 1980.

The generation of the 1960s grew up with Vietnam, Mahayana Buddhists from China, and Zen and Theravadian Buddhists from Southeast Asia. The Vietnamese Buddhists became visible participants in the war that afflicted their country. On May 11, 1963, their plight came to the attention of the general public with the self-immolation of Thich Quang Duc in Saigon. Self-immolation was a rarely used Buddhist practice engaged in only by those who had reached the highest state of meditative perfection. It was used as an act of martyrdom in Saigon to draw attention to the fact that over twenty thousand Buddhist monks had been rounded up to be killed by the government. The image of Thich Quang Duc, hands clasped in a mudra (Buddhist hand gesture) and his body ablaze, became a symbol of the anguish of the war. The horrifying scene was dramatically brought to American homes via newspapers, magazines, and television.

By the late 1960s more than a score of Zen Buddhist groups, inspired by Soyen Shaku, Sokei-an, Senzaki, and D.T. Suzuki, had opened centers for learning and meditation. In New York, the First Zen Institute moved into a brownstone on East Thirtieth Street under the leadership of Mary Farkas, whose *Zen Notes* kept track of the emerging scene. In 1967, the Reverend Nakajima, a young priest who had studied in Ceylon, sat *zazen* on the Upper West Side. There were Zen groups in Philadelphia, Boston, Washington, Chicago, San Francisco, and Hawaii. In 1968, a group incorporated itself as the Zen Center of Los Angeles. Youth of the 1960s made their way to the Soto Zen Mission in San Francisco to sit zazen. Tai Shemano-sansei began meeting in 1964 with a small group in a practice room at the American Buddhist Academy in New York. He had known D.T. Suzuki while Suzuki was at Columbia, where he taught John Cage and others. In 1965, Philip Kapleau returned to the U.S. after 13 years in Japan, where he had published *The Three Pillars of Zen.* Chester and Doris Carlson read the book, were impressed and invited Kapleau to visit with them in Rochester. The following year, Kapleau founded the Zen Meditation Center. Gradually, Kapleau westernized his zendo with English versions of sutras and western style dress designed for sitting comfort. He asked Yasutani-roshi to translate the *Heart Sutra* into English in order to make it more accessible to Americans. On July 4, 1976, *sesshin* from all over the world came to the Catskills in New York State to mark the opening of Dai Bosatsu, the first traditional Japanese style Zen monastery in America.

Publications such as the *San Francisco Oracle* included the ideas of Walt Whitman, American Indians, Shiva, Kali, Buddha, tarot, astrology, Zen, and Tantra. They printed the *Heart Sutra* with a two-page spread about the Los Angeles Zen Center; the pages were decorated with psychedelic borders and naked goddesses. Gary Snyder, Allen Ginsberg, Lawrence Ferlinghetti, and Michael McClure, met at the first " Be-In" at Golden Gate Park. Shunryu-roshi appeared briefly, holding a single flower, along with Timothy Leary and Richard Alpert. Leary, a former Harvard professor, had recast the verses of the *Tao Te Ching* into a book called *Psychedelic Prayers* and had taken the *Bhardo Thodol, the Tibetan Book of The Dead*, as a guidebook. Influenced by Leary, many participants took LSD in the belief that they would become clearer about the sutras, the *Bhagavad Gita*, and their inner beings.

In the midst of the Vietnam war, race riots, inflation, drugs, and political demonstrations, many artists of the late 1960s and the 1970s searched for alternative art forms and alternative concepts. In a society of materialism and war, they expressed their disdain for objects and for Western traditions. In order to reach a higher reality, they turned to Eastern philosophical ideas for aesthetic solutions. They read Lao Tzu's *Tao Te Ching* and studied the *I-Ching*. Some came to these texts indirectly through phenomenology and the writings of Maurice Merleau-Ponty. Influenced by the writings of Alan Watts, D.T. Suzuki, Eugen Herrigel, Allen Ginsberg, Gary Snyder, Jack Kerouac and Robert Pirsig's *Zen and the Art of Motorcycle Maintenance*, the music of John Cage and the art of Mark Tobey, Morris Graves, Ad Reinhardt and Isamu Noguchi, the artists of the late 1960s and the 1970s developed an art that was intuitive, "purposeless" and in direct response to their perception of their surrounding space. The artists of this generation came to feel that Western society had succeeded in ensuring physical comfort through technology but had neglected spiritual needs. Pollution, industrialization, technology and materialism presented spiritual problems, and European rationalism and science no longer seemed to have all of the solutions. Americans were looking for alternatives, for a "reality" other than that which was verifiable by the senses. In the process of shaping their ideas, these artists moved from "realism," an imitation of physical reality, to "realization," a direct perception of *Reality*. Their work illustrates evolving states of consciousness. Asian philosophy, particularly Zen (as it was popularized in the West during the 1960s) promised a new approach, a new outlook on *Reality*.

The ideas that artists found in Far Eastern philosophies such as Buddhism, Taoism, and Zen offered a new way of looking at the world. They melded these ideas into a perspective in which the soul of man/woman was seen as a *Void* and one's identity as a series of moments of consciousness surrounding the *Void*.

Fig. 24. Carl Andre, *Pyre* 1961
Western red cedar
48 x 36 x 36"
Collection of Sondra and Charles Gilman, Jr.

The *Void* is the *Nothingness* that is charged with energy or the life force, "*chi*." It is the white spaces in a painting, the pause in music, the hub of a wheel. The *Void* is space that is empty but not vacant. It evokes not loneliness or despair but contemplation. It is the inner self.

Artists created icons which could become one with the *Void* — a *Void* replete with life's energies. Within this *Void* are *Yin* and *Yang*, representing all the opposites — feminine/masculine, dark/light, negative/posi-

tive, passive/aggressive. They created simple, passive, transparent, uncarved forms with unlimited potential. Because unnecessary elements have been eliminated, both the artist and the viewer-turned-participant begin to intuitively grasp *Reality*. The art points the way to self-realization. This art plays with our perception of things. It forces our mind to move beyond the surface forms. Like the artist, the potter for a tea ceremony wants the Zen student to understand what he has done: to see the clay, to feel and admire its texture, to appreciate the form and the glaze. He draws our attention to the original elements and to a process that is made to seem effortless. In a haiku, simple lines capture intersections of the timeless and the ephemeral. Love in haiku is directed toward nature as much as toward a man or woman. A flower arrangement is to a large garden what a haiku is to an epic poem — an abbreviated form which suggests the larger world.

In the 1960s and 1970s, many artists chose to reduce their format to the essentials and thereby discover and achieve a deeper understanding of themselves. They came to realize that all art begins with a blank canvas, a lump of clay, or a raw piece of stone the artist enlivens it with "*chi.*" The blank space or unformed mass, the *Emptiness* or spiritual solid, is ready to receive anything — it has unlimited potential. Many of the art objects created become a source of contemplation and changes that occur in the basic form and in the mind of the viewer. The form directs the viewer/participant to understand the Emptiness; and what we see is what we are.

The transparent thread that binds the art of the period from 1965 to 1985 is an alternative world view that was explored in the work of the Pop and Funk artists and experienced by such artists as Bruce Nauman, Carl Andre, Robert Morris, Richard Serra, Michael Singer, Michelle Stuart, Patricia Johanson, Christopher Wilmarth, Eric Orr, and Robert Irwin. It is also found in the work of Sol LeWitt, James Turrell, Keith Sonnier, Robert Smithson, and many others of varied sensibility, styles and form.[1] The subject is the *Path*, the *Tao*; the forms are only the expressions of the struggle to attain the experience.

Bruce Nauman left the California Funk scene and bridged the gap between his teachers, Robert Arneson and William Wiley, and the Minimalists and Conceptual artists. He sought to obliterate the distinction between "high" art, and a "low" art which uses pop-culture objects. He moved from demystifying objects of popular culture to eliminating the object altogether. While at the University of California at Davis in 1965, Nauman worked with Wiley to create the *Slant Step* (Fig.4 ). Many works of art were subsequently created concerning this "found object," which had no use. As Nauman said, "it was something that everybody thought had a function until you really tried to use it." His next works dealt with the spaces between objects. Nauman sought to reveal the truths about these spaces, the *Voids*. He cast the space under a chair or beneath a shelf. He would penetrate the empty spaces with sounds such as those of exhaling breaths or of pounding or laughing.

Wiley and Arneson were important influences for Nauman and the next generation of artists through both their teachings and their art. Arneson's involvement with Zen has been clearly demonstrated. He has said of Zen, "It was around everywhere. You had to have been dead not to have been exposed to it." As pointed out

earlier, Wiley has expressed similar thoughts.[2] Nauman explored the ideas inherent in Asian philosophy through film, sculpture, installations, environments, performances, video, and sound. In the mid-1970s he created works that consisted of a set of written instructions to be followed. For example, in his "centering piece," viewers/participants enter a room with a high ceiling and are instructed to go to the center of the room and locate its center, somewhere above eye level. The viewer is then instructed to locate his/her own center and move it until it coincides with the room's center. Nauman is interested in "what is not there" and in solving "impossible" problems, like the ancient "one hand clapping" koan. He is concerned with the battle between consciousness and perception, between what is known and what is seen, and between illusion and reality, and with the struggle to know.

In his *Window/Wall Sign* (Fig.61) , Nauman made visible the quest of the artists of this period. This peach and blue neon work created in 1965 contains words which form a spiral that moves at once inward and outward. It is meant to be placed in a window so that the words can be read easily from the outside, and yet from the inside looking out it is difficult to discern the words. In the same way, the artist looking out from his inner being sometimes has difficulty understanding his role, while the viewer of the art begins see to the artist's inner psyche. From the inside of the spiral outward, the piece reads, "The true artist helps the world by revealing mystic truths." The poetic message spirals out as if it were going on endlessly. When seen from the inside the message is confusing because it is reversed and inverted.

Nauman is not interested in adding to "the things that are art" but in "investigating what art may be."[3] In 1966, he created a pink mylar window shade that reads, "The true artist is an amazing luminous fountain." Some of the letters are painted, some are scratched in. This led to a piece the following year titled *Self Portrait as Fountain*, which shows Nauman from the waist up spouting water into the air. Both these works are ambiguous and yet loaded with meaning and references. They hark back to Duchamp's *Fountain* (a urinal he placed on exhibit as a "readymade") and to the Taoist maxim of "*wu wei,*" which is the stream which is always moving and in a state of flux capable of breaking down stone. Wiley noted that "for me Duchamp was Zen," and this idea was surely conveyed to his student Nauman. Indeed, Nauman was influenced by Duchamp, but it was more than Duchamp–it was a continued concern with attitude, with changes in the perception of space, a new awareness of the relationship between form and void, and a re-evaluation of the "role" of the artist.

Many other artists looked to Asian philosophy as a way to deal with experience, space, and alternative perceptions. Carl Andre is one of many artists who admits to having been influenced by one of the most important

Eastern philosophical texts, the *Tao Te Ching*. This text captured the essence of Taoism, the *Void* and the balance of opposites. In 1961, Andre displayed *Pyre* (Fig.24) blocks of wood which he left uncarved. By displaying unworked material as sculpture, Andre proposed that the viewer sensed the object's physical existence as an aesthetic phenomenon. *Pu*, the Uncarved Block, is a critical symbol in Taoism and Zen philosophy. It denotes the natural state of viewing, simplicity, purity, and infinite potentiality. Andre displayed many variations of his Uncarved Blocks. One series consisted of two to five 36 inch beams of western red cedar standing and lying on the floor in all four directions, reaching out to all the corners of the universe while the center remained empty. The Art is the act of selecting and placing things, unveiling the uncarved block. Andre's work exists only while we look at it as art. After the exhibition, the pieces of wood or brick or copper are stacked, stored and returned to their status as mundane objects. There is a very fragile relationship between these objects and art: a transitory relationship, provisional, tenuous, impermanent. There is no longer a division between subject and object. This impermanence is called *anicca* in Buddhism. It is like all life, transitory and in a constant state of flux.

This Asian philosophical concept of change is most profoundly expressed in the *I-Ching* or *Book of Changes*, written in about 500 B.C. This text and its concepts of change and chance, silence and simplicity, were critical to many artists, including John Cage, Carl Andre, and Walter De Maria. The *I-Ching*, characterized by the character "*I*," is usually simplified in translations as "change." More elaborate definitions are found in the character combination of sun and moon (*Yin* and *Yang*). The most literal meaning of "*I*" is easy, simple, understated. The emphasis in this book is to view life as simple. The *I-Ching* says, among other things, "What is easy, is easy to know."

Another central element of the *I-Ching* is that "change is the unchangeable." Artists such as John Cage were particularly influenced by the concepts in the *I-Ching*. The *I-Ching* was one such teacher along with D.T. Suzuki's lessons on Zen.[4] Cage's music and art embody the spirit of *I-Ching*. Beginning with a simple structure, he combines positive and negative space or sounds that constantly change within a format left to chance.

Walter De Maria was knowledgeable about the *I-Ching*, and reveals his admiration for John Cage in an early sculpture he created titled *Statue for John Cage*. He sent a photograph of the piece with a note to Cage, but barely contacted the musician beyond that tribute. De Maria's first interest was music. In his musical compositions, such as "Ocean and Drums," he showed Cage's influence in the seemingly unchanging monotonic beating of drums, with a barely audible sound of the ocean in the background. At a certain point the

ocean seems to take over. De Maria worked with LaMonte Young, a musician who was also profoundly influenced by Eastern philosophy. In Young's music, sequences of single notes were held for a long period without any apparent variations, yet the sounds changed as our perception of them changed.

De Maria's art has different layers of meaning. Such works as *High Energy Bar* (Fig.42) or *Bronze Column* (Fig.43) appear to be simple, beautifully polished, static forms. The column reminds us of Brancusi's *Endless Column* and becomes the infinite continuity of space and time. The *High Energy Bar* is accompanied by a certificate stating that the piece belongs forever to the owner. Only his death can break the tie. The owner can never rid himself of the bar. The piece suddenly has its own continuity in time. And what is a "high energy bar?" The words are clearly stamped on its side, but they reveal nothing of its function. De Maria has left us with a koan — an unanswerable question.

De Maria's *Hexagon* (Fig.44) is a stainless steel form which lies on the floor. A channel holds a ball which the viewer/participant can move. This idea of the viewer as participant is reminiscent of De Maria's earlier sculpture, *Boxes for Meaningless Work* (1961), which instructed the individual to move a ball from one place to another. These works also resemble Brecht's "game sculptures," which required audience participation.[5] The sculpture is never static. The sculpture is about change but what is one to make of the title? A hexagon has six sides, but De Maria's form ... even. If we look to the *I-Ching* perhaps we find ...

The *I-Ching* or *Bo...* oracle book as well as a philosoph... ...grams made up of six broke... ...s and commentaries. These li... ...f action and change. The b... ...gative, passive, weak, do... ...ive, active, strong). The... ...ces are always inter... ...e one constant in life ... ...change. Through simpli... ...reveal life's constant change. In *360° I-Ching*, ...e Maria actually reconstructed all 64 hexagrams on the floor out of stainless steel rods (Fig.25,26).

There are six hexagrams in the *I-Ching* which consist of five solid lines and one broken line (Fig.25). If we look at DeMaria's *Hexagon* (Fig.44), we realize that one side is not symmetrical and appears to be a straight line that has been bent or broken. This would account for a six-sided hexagram having seven sides: one side is a broken line. If one side is a broken line, the form can then represent any one of the following:[6]

Hsiao Ch'u (the taming power of the small)
Li (treading-conduct) (difference between high and low)
Tung Jen (fellowship with men)
Ta Yu (possession in great measure)
Kuai (breakthrough, resoluteness)
Kuo (coming to meet)

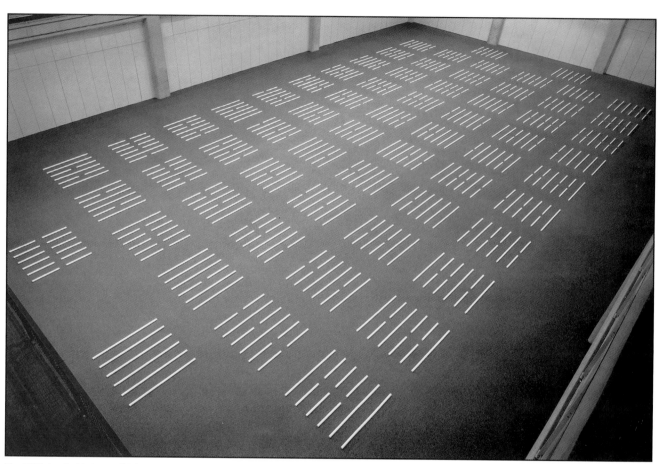

Fig. 25 Walter De Maria, *360° I Ching/64 Sculptures*, 1981
Collection Dia Art Foundation, NY
Photo credit: Nic Tenwiggenhorn

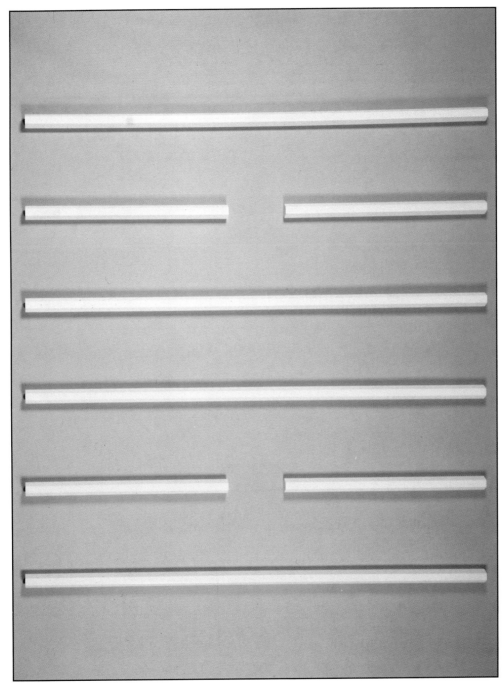

Fig. 26 Walter De Maria, *360o I Ching/64 Sculptures*, 1981, Detail
Collection Dia Art Foundation, NY
Photo credit: Tord Lund

In each of these, which have various interpretations, the *Yin* or more passive element begin to change and take over *Yang*. Significantly in this work, the ball which can move represents the change. The center of the form is empty, for it embodies in its *Nothingness* all possible change and the balancing of *Yin* and *Yang*.

Robert Morris explicates these ideas in his art and his writings. His article titled "The Present Tense of Space" (1978) on the Japanese art of swordsmithing explains the perennial balance of contradictions in life.

> The sword was the primary side arm before the perfection of the flintlock. For centuries two types of swords were made. Those tempered soft were flexible but held no cutting edge. Those tempered hard held an edge but were brittle and easily broken. The idea of a good sword was a contradiction in terms until around the 11th century when the Japanese brought the mutually exclusive together by forging a sheath of hard steel over a core of softer temper.[7]

He ends the article with the words, "The pursuit of the contradictory, be it in art or sword-making, is the only basis for perceiving dialectical reality." This perception of reality as the melding of the contradictory is a constant theme in Morris' work. The direct perception of the *T'ai Chi*, which is composed of the *Yin* and *Yang*, is his ultimate goal. A balance is struck between clarity and confusion, between *Yin* and *Yang*. Morris says he wanted to provide "an experience of an interaction between the perceiving body and the world which fully admits that the terms of this interaction are temporal as well as spatial, that existence is process, that art itself is a form of behavior."[8] His felt pieces balance the regular cuts of the felt against the way they fall, irregularly and by chance (Fig.58). Interested in the phenomenology of Maurice Merleau-Ponty, Morris aimed at creating:

> ...a place in which the perceiving self might take measure of certain aspects of its own physical existence... Have we become less concerned with absolutes, with our place in the universe and with our own individual mortality? In some sense I believe we have. It has not just been an exhaustion of modernist forms. An emotional weariness with what underlies them has occurred. I would suggest that the shift has occurred with the growing awareness of the more global threats to the existence of life itself...Perhaps we can all become Zen masters. After all, Zen originated as a martial discipline which enabled the samurai to become indifferent toward his own demise.[9]

From the mid-1960s to the early 1970s there was an intense interplay between Morris and other artists such as Andre, LeWitt, Smithson, and De Maria.[10] They worked and influenced each other. Morris' first major sculptural piece was *Box with Sound of its Own Making* (1961) (Fig.27), which contained within the box a recording of the making of the box. In this work, the process of mak-

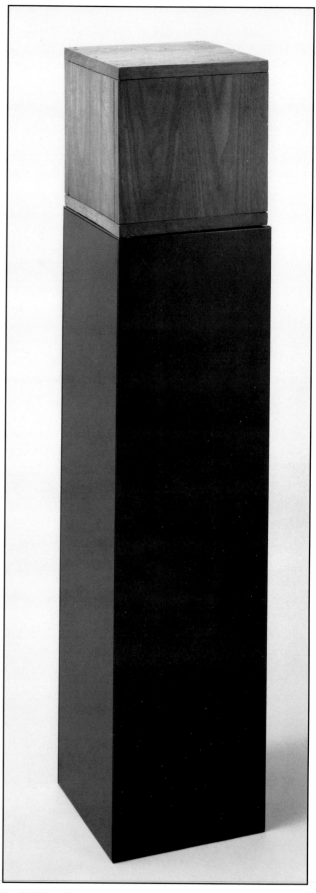

Fig. 27 Robert Morris, Box *With Sound Of Its Own Making* 1961-78
Seattle Art Museum, Gift of Bagley and Virginia Wright 82.190

ing the cube seems to go on endlessly, and the maker of the box seems trapped inside in this continuous process. The mindlessness is enlightened mindlessness, like Zen. As John Cage stated, in *Silences* (1966)[11], the contemporary mind has learned to "turn the tables and see meaninglessness as ultimate meaning." This box was followed by the *I Box*, which contained, a photograph of the naked artist. These boxes were followed by his "grey boxes," which contain no specific sound or image inside but rather his own presence in a primary form. The soul of the artist is the Void in the box, as he is reintegrated into that Void. His work is about the space of the self within.

Morris' "mirror" series began to appear in 1961. They reduce the power of the geometric forms. These mirrored cubes appear to change constantly, depending on what is in the room. The process of making the piece into a work of art to be viewed is now also dependent on the viewer, who becomes a participant. They reflect everything in the room. They seem formless yet they occupy space. A change in position changes perspective and changes the box. The mirrored box is like the Zen mind: it can never be wiped clean, for it always reflects, though it possesses nothing. Is it reality or illusion? For Morris, reductive modernism is a way to reach Nirvana. Somewhere deep in this mirror realm, a vestigial self of the artist lives.

In 1970, Richard Serra, working in the Bronx, where he was surrounded by burnt-out remnants of buildings, created *To Encircle Base Plate Hexagram, Right Angles Inverted* (Fig.28). He implanted a twenty-six foot steel circle into an asphalt street. Half of the circle had a wide flange, the other half a narrow one. Like the buildings around, it became the remnants of lives and ideas. The flange of each semicircle was akin to the *Yin* and *Yang* of the *T'ai Chi*. Serra admits that a trip to Japan with Carl Andre had had a great impact on him, and his knowledge of Eastern philosophy. The word "Hexagram" in the title of the piece refers back to the *I-Ching* and the idea of change. The piece may even be viewed as a "Buddhist garden", to be perused, studied, and contemplated.

Serra created his first urban outdoor piece in 1970, in Ueno Park in Tokyo. That work consisted of two inverted rings. A second, rectilinear work, made in the Kyoto National Museum, was comprised of one part on the ground and one in the ground. In an interview with Douglas Crimp in 1980 (*Arts* 1980), Serra noted that, later that year he built the piece at 183rd Street and Webster Avenue in the Bronx (fig.28), using the same vocabulary.

> After looking for a site in the Bronx for three or four months, I found a dead-end street that had stairways going up to an adjacent street, which would enable a viewer to look down on the piece from various levels. 183rd was a left-over street in a broken-down neighborhood, unencumbered by buildings; it had no public or institutional character. The only nearby housing was about a block away. Except for wrecked cars, there were empty lots and open space...The place in the Bronx was sinister, used by the local criminals to torch the cars they'd stolen. There was no audience for the scupture in the Bronx, and it was my misconception that the so-called art audience would seek the work out. But even in being problematic the work in the Bronx clarified the issue. In the development of my urban work this piece remains important.

It explicated the idea that no site is neutral.

In the Hindu and Buddhist temples, the stupa outside represents the center of the universe. It is supposed to be circumambulated by the viewer/participant and understood from each direction. Similarly, Serra's *Prop* pieces (Fig.71) carefully and tenuously are the *Yin* and *Yang*, opposites balanced between the outside and inside, the societal and the philosophical, displaying the instability of forms, balanced by a central energy or force.

Oriental art has also been a major influence on Michael Singer's art and way of life. Singer creates visual tensions, like the Chinese polarities of *Yin* and *Yang*; his structures are fluent and flexible and yet express a sense of wholeness. Even Singer's indoor works, with their precarious balance, are reminiscent of the precarious balance in nature, a balance that is the key to the harmony of the universe. Like the *T'ai Chi*, Singer's works seem to balance opposing forces and to redirect energy.

Between 1975 and 1980, Singer began to use stones as a foundation and as a structural element.

> I sense these stones as symbols containing references to mountains, river, cloud, natural elements. I take long walks to look for stones that come from walls, fields and streams. Once I have the stones I place them in the studio where I spend a long time determining which edges should be cut. I categorize the stones visually — vertical, horizontal, diagonal, round, sharp, weathered by the air, time honored.[11]

Singer's work, like the Zen garden, manifests *sabi* (the patina of time) and *wabi* (understatement). In *First Gate Ritual*, the stones he uses, as in a Japanese garden, are full of their own history and mythology. Stone is, of course, often used as a symbol of the eternal (Fig.29). Singer particularly likes to use slate and granite. Slate is formed when layers of silt laden with vegetation and organisms are subjected to heat and pressure. Traces of silt are left in the imperfections of the slate, making it seem more "alive." Granite, formed from molten matter deep in the earth, is, according to Singer, "the most enduring and stable stone."[12] If nature is grasped as a process rather than an object, "then the work's shifting definition within the equilibrium of the atmosphere provides a means of being a part of it, linking man and environment through the action of making."[13] Singer has tried to condense the universe into a single

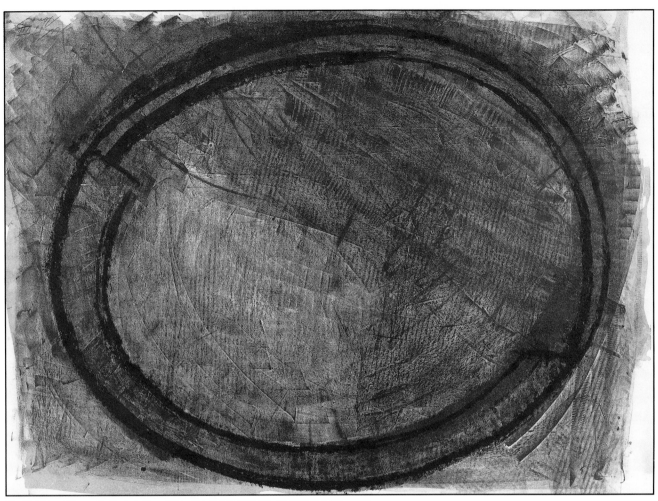

Fig. 28 Richard Serra, *To Encircle Base Plate, Hexagram 183rd St. and Webster Ave.* 1972
Collection, The Museum of Modern Art, New York
Gift of Leo and Jean-Christophe Castelli in memory of Toiny Castelli

span, like a Japanese garden. The rocks at the Ryoan-ji temple, for example, were especially chosen to represent mountains and crags. The gardener looked not so much for odd shapes but for ones that seemed authoritative and monumental. Each possessed a weathered texture, displaying centuries of wear. Ryoan-ji goes beyond a symbolic representation of a landscape to a distillation of the universe. The empty areas both emphasize the stones and invite the mind to expand in the cosmological infinity that they suggest. The interaction between form and space is important. Evoking a sense of infinity in a strictly confined space, it is a lesson in Zen Nothingness and Non-Attachment. It expresses a timelessness inspiring contemplation.

Singer's recent work is a low structure reminiscent of a Buddhist gate or Shinto shrine. Nearly twenty feet long, it fills a large cavernous space. We are drawn through the space to a natural Void. The density of the forms distend into space. The rhythms of the forms seem to contradict themselves. The viewer circumambulates the sculpture trying to capture different segments and compositions. As the piece and the pro-

cess of viewing it unfold, the viewer becomes explicitly and implicitly a part of it. Singer is constantly adjusting his sculptures to suit the environment. Singer notes the changes in wind, water, clouds and light and that every moment will be different. Landscape in Asian art has always referred to the endless change and flux of man's environment. Singer's work represents an escape from industrialization to nature. It is concerned with the subtleties of changing landscapes, with their tenuous balance of elements.

A participant may touch a stone or witness the wind moving the piece, altering this fragile balance. In other works he has used reeds and bamboo structures rather than other woods, such as oak, in accordance with the Oriental tenet of the inherent strength of these materials, because they sway and bend in the breeze, yielding to natural forces instead of fighting them. Donald Kuspit said of Singer's work, "The sculpture's flexibility has a didactic point. It suggests the Taoist maxim that recommends, at certain moments, life as a bamboo rather than an oak — bamboo that bends with the big wind and thereby survives it."[14]

Fig. 29 Michael Singer, *Ritual Series 5/84* 1984
Courtesy Sperone, Westwater, Inc.

Singer approaches nature as an object not to conquer "but to meet as a friendly, well meaning agent whose inner being is thoroughly like our own."[15] He does not impose himself on nature, but works in areas of unspoiled land, on projects that would surely be ruined if the usual flock of gallery patrons trooped out en masse to view them. To find his outdoor pieces requires a conscious effort on the part of the observer; a retreat to nature in search of a revelation about the universe is an integral part of Taoism and Zen. It was in nature that a person could have a revelation about his own being and his place within that universe. Through the "veil" of nature one could come to have a greater understanding of reality.

> I wanted (the art) to look accidental, unintended, as though a work of nature. There was to be no human presence; perhaps because I was still trying to understand what my own presence in this natural environment should be. It became an absolute rule that there should be no sign of human presence. Part of my obsession about the absence of humans in these works came from the shame I feel about being part of a culture that has systematically destroyed the natural environment. Western culture views man at the top, controlling nature, apart from it...In order to experience and learn from the natural environment I felt the need to yield to it, respect it, to observe, to learn and then work with it. This early rule that I had, to not allow my presence in the work, was helpful in this yielding and learning process. Eventually, I accepted my role in the environment as more than observer, manager, researcher. I understood this role as artist.[16]

Eugen Herrigel in *Zen and The Art of Archery* explains that true art is purposeless. Zen advises its followers to deal directly with the object, become one with it and "shoot from within." By becoming one with nature, the artist or the archer can achieve his/her goal. In Zen there is no separation between subject and object. The aim of Zen is to restore the experience of original inseparability, to return to the original state of purity and transparency.

Many of the artists of the last quarter-century have found the paradigm of "wholeness" and the perfect balance of forces already existing in nature. They have used nature, the flowers, rocks, light and space as a model for their art. They seek to preserve the balance that humanity frequently destroys. Artists, such as Michelle Stuart and Patricia Johanson as well as Michael Singer and Eric Orr, create a microcosm of that macrocosm. They emphasize the Asian belief in the sacred quality of nature. They become a small part of that myriad of forces, and they create works that seek to capture the Totality of Nature. Emerson's comments are apt. "Instead of the sublime and beautiful; the near, the low, the common was explored and poeticized. That which had been negligently trodden under foot by those who were harnessing a provision for themselves for the long journey into far countries, is suddenly found to be richer than all foreign parts."[17]

Michelle Stuart incorporates nature into her art by gathering fragments and capturing their interchange. Since 1972 she has used rocks and minerals to make natural history more tangible, and she has created scrolls and books (Fig.73) in which the earth is rubbed into the paper. The books, carefully bound, seem old and worn. They have a patina of time; they have become histories without words. The seemingly blank pages are laden with potential. The books are to be understood without opening them or going through a time sequence. She frequently refers to the Thousand Buddha Caves, which contain sacred texts but have been sealed so that no one can view them. The secrets are kept; the options limitless.

Stuart has been interested in religions since high school, and has accumulated a library of books on religions and philosophies of the Far East. Amidst texts on Taoism, is a copy of the *Koma Sutra*, the *I-Ching* and *Tibetan Book of the Dead*. She has studied the writings of D.T. Suzuki, Watts, and Christmas Humphrey, *The Teaching of the Buddha* and has a Zen dictionary for reference. In the 1960s, she was a follower of the Maharishi, Stuart meditates and does yoga. She is a product of her generation but as an artist has been able to express the most profound of the ideas she has studied and to transform them into a format which allows her to share the Asian outlook on life with Western society. Her paintings contain a talismanic spirit. They are like the petals of a lotus flower, concealing when closed, opening and revealing for a brief moment for those who wait.[18]

In the early 1980s, Stuart began a series of paintings in which she used earth pigments and beeswax, creating large textured paintings in which are embedded stones, fossils, earth and pigments. She conceived of them in relation to Buddhism's Eightfold Path to Self-Enlightenment.[19]

The compositions are divided into grids, which order the nature on the canvas and provide a sequence of time. Each section is a fragment of the whole, each a microcosm of the macrocosm. Like a Zen student, Stuart pays careful attention to the most minute details:

a stone, the earth, a fossil. *Sabi I* (Fig.22) at first seems like a field of muted grey and silver, but within the field are the details. Understatement and restraint are obvious qualities of her work. As in Zen, the artist holds something in reserve in order to entice the viewer to look beyond the surface. It does not yield all of its secrets in the first viewing; like an Ad Reinhart "black painting," Stuart's painting requires prolonged viewing to reveal all its nuances.

Stuart's works are about the passage of time or *sabi*, the patina of time. She builds her art with layers of time, space and forms. She has said, "The earth leaves traces of time...We imprint and are imprints of all that came before. Anticipating future."[20] She has traveled to Japan and Southeast Asia to learn about their cultural traditions, merging prehistory and modernism, and like the *I-Ching,* her art is about change. As in the *Tao Te Ching* she regards nature as a whole and the essence, the mutable, transient, and infinite. In her journal, Stuart reflects on meaning in her art.

> Rubbing and polishing stones is an ancient activity of human kind...dreamers innermost being...true personality. Stones hidden in caves, wrapped in bark...containers of divine powers...rub stones...power increases...(charged with electricity)...vibrations from the place (site) send them back with ours. Shape the stone...Stone is Self...return stone to land...part of soul remains. We are all part of a whole, no good/bad facile dualisms...all one pulsating force.[21]

Stuart's work can be compared to this Taoist passage

> ...if Nature is to be loved, it must be caught while moving....Let us destroy all artificial barriers we put up between Nature and ourselves, for it is only when they are removed that we see into the living heart of Nature and live with it.[22]

In Patricia Johanson's early works, she sought to capture the essence of nature through a single stroke on a canvas (Fig.45 ), or a line of slate in the landscape, but as her work evolved she found the perfect example in nature itself. "I have been interested in the Orient for as long as I can remember," she said. "My mother took me to the Brooklyn Botanical Garden and its Japanese Garden when I was a child...and now I own so many books relating to the Orient, it's obvious that their ideas and designs strike a responsive chord."[23]

Johanson has visited Japan and participated in religious ceremonies at Kokadera Temple. She has visited Japanese gardens, read haiku poetry, and the sutras, has been to the Chinese opera, and has taken Karate. She conveys Far Eastern culture through an art form that reintegrates man with nature in an ever changing spectrum of infinite forms. She collected rocks in order to make her own rock gardens, and she has observed the reflections, the shadows, and the water that

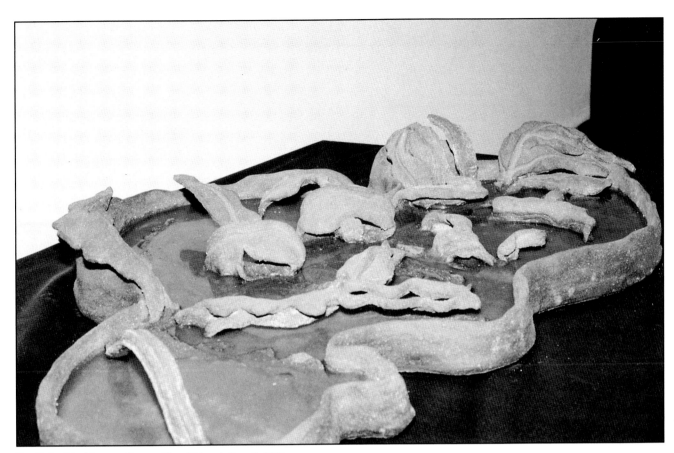

Fig. 30. Patricia Johanson, *Drowned Fern (Polypody Fern III)* 1980
Courtesy the Artist

changed the personality of the rock. Johanson's works embody many of these ideas. They are about changes, life, death and growth, and they endeavor to bring us closer to who we are and our place in the universe.

Johanson's work is based on the traditional Asian garden. The garden is rarely designed to be seen all at once or from one viewpoint; rather, like the Sung landscape scroll painting, which is to be opened in small sections and contemplated, the viewer slowly follows a path. The garden is ever changing, because each viewer brings to it his or her own perceptions. In *The Book of Tea*, Kakuzo Okakuro stressed that true beauty could be discovered only when the viewer completed the incomplete.[24] The garden captures your attention until you seem to become a part of it — you fill the empty space. "The vacant space of the garden, like silence, absorbs the mind, frees it of petty detail, and serves as a visual guide — a means for penetrating through the `realm of multitudes.'"[25] It is the rocks at Ryoan-ji that define the emptiness; without them we have no point of reference. Similarly, the spokes or the outer rim of a wheel realizes the hub or empty space of the wheel, and sounds define silence. White expanses in a painting, a pause in poetry, a break in a dance are pregnant with experiences.

While at Bennington College, Johanson took a course in comparative religion and was impressed by

the *Tao Te Ching* by Lao Tzu, and by the teachings of the Buddha. She still has her old copy of *Tao Te Ching* and in it has underlined twice the phrase, "The way of nature...is the process and not static. The way is not the path which nature might take, but is the movement of nature itself; it is an effortless movement...like the annual rhythm of the seasons."[26] Those words echo throughout Johanson's *oeuvre*.

In 1960, Johanson wrote about redesigning the world as a work of art.[27] She suggested creating a total environmental design which involved not only aesthetic concerns, but also ecological, sociological and psychological interests as well"..."to use aesthetics as a living organic form."[28]

Johanson bases her designs on elements from the land and the natural cycles of life and death which they embody. Her use of ferns is an excellent example. Johanson explains:

> I had picked these ferns and wanted them to be perfect. I would leave them on the drawing table and would keep throwing them away because the ferns had shriveled and died. I then started to draw them in whatever state they were. Suddenly it was not just a fern, it was like a person, and you could translate the suffering. There is a whole series which starts with one perfect fern; then the mouse came and made holes in it: then it shriveled and

was like an old person. (The veins of the fern had gone from front to back and they begin protruding in different ways just like in older people). Finally the fern disintegrated and became translated back into the landscape. This is very Oriental because they believe that the Universe is all one piece and that they can look at anything and translate it into anything else. I do the same thing. I only look at a few things. Every time I see my Grandmother, for example, I see her body changing. I see her body becoming a landscape. It is preparing to go back into the earth. It is turning from a structure with a purpose to bones and protruding arteries. I want to be able to translate this fern into something universal...As the ferns shriveled up, I began to see them as so much more than they were. They were beautiful stretched out and green one day, and then they fell apart — so I drew the little pieces. My son thought they were ugly and took them out and threw them in a mud puddle, and they were mostly under water, so then I drew them just like that, lying there in the mud puddle...The real creativity is in daily life.[29]

Johanson made the fern into a fountain (Fig. 30), revealing the macrocosm by dealing with the microcosm. In *Snake in the Grass* for Phillip Glass, another fountain, the flow of water changes how much of the snakes are revealed. This series of two images (Figs. 46, 47) shows nature and art as process. There is a sense of timelessness in this work. It is also *Tathata*, seeing things as they really are, revealing their true nature, eliminating the boundaries between subject and object.

In 1981, Johanson was asked to submit a proposal for the redesigning of the Dallas Fair Park Lagoon (now called the Leonhardt Lagoon). In the proposal, which resulted in a commissioned project, she wrote about creating an environment which would reunite man and nature (Fig.19). She based the entire design on the image of an indigenous flower. In order for the art work to become the instigator of the viewer's experience, Johanson designed an open-ended structure, which, like nature, was adaptable and flexible. The water lilies exemplify the transience of the piece: in the morning they open, but by two in the afternoon they have closed and the entire lagoon has changed.

Johanson's art is functional, aesthetic and public. A "totalization" of space is achieved by her division of space. Her simultaneous use of large and small scale presents the viewer/participant with the macrocosm and the microcosm. "It is the vast configuration versus personal confrontation with any of an infinite number of intimate details."[30] The single focus is replaced by multiple foci, so that viewing becomes a personal experience — a key element in classical Chinese landscape painting and Zen.[31]

Robert Irwin feels that his predisposition to Zen came out of his earlier fascination with cars, spending hours polishing surfaces that no one would even see (such as the undergirdings of the dashboard).[33] Irwin has also noted that Robert Pirsig's *Zen and the Art of Motorcycle Maintenance* was a source for him of the blending of Oriental philosophy and Western technology, a revelation. "I mean, a motorcycle can be a lot more than just a machine that runs along; it can be a whole description of a personality and an aesthetic."[34] And he later wrote, "The Zen stuff was just reinforcing something I'd learned long before while working on my cars."[35]

Irwin has become best known for his art of empty spaces. As a "Light and Space" artist, he sought to embody the *Nothingness*. Irwin experimented with anarchoic chambers and escapes to deserted lands. Robert Irwin's most successful early series of works were his "disc paintings," which succeeded in breaking the barrier of the edge of the canvas. Four tangential white discs, resting on a white wall, come together and dissolve into space. The affect is experiential, so illustrations are useless. Irwin wrote about this alternative art form:

> Radical change in our lives, occurs when the methods of our time-worn practices, checked and rechecked, are unable to account for a growing accumulation of instances and questions to the contrary; and we are forced to go deeper (to expose our hidden orthodoxies)...we need to attain an uncommitted bare-bones ground where we can ask, how might it be otherwise? And to gain ground, we can only begin by confronting our own beliefs...my first hint (intuition) that the world of my perceptual and aesthetic concerns might not begin and end at the edge of my canvas was something that had no tangible reality...And is not the idea of a non-object art a contradiction in terms? What would this art be made of? Where would it exist? And how would we come to know it, let alone judge it? Yet again, if we are to continue to take the words "aesthetics" and "perception" as having serious bearing on art, can we simply continue to hold the dialogue of art to be subsumable to the making of objects?
>
> ...For my generation, to regain the necessary balance to pursue the process of peeling back the layers of our world — i.e., to deal with the questions posed by non-objective art - certain things needed to be kept in focus...ideas (questions are meaningless unless we let them affect (change) our lives)...this process is not in itself a negative one, that the old concepts are not in themselves untrue, only that they have become incapable of satisfying our extended questioning. But here, in this desert, we can now begin to question how it might be otherwise.[32]

Perception is a key concept in the understanding of Irwin's art. He breaks through the traditional boundaries of art, such as the frame, in order to get us to focus on the environment, the surroundings and the space. Irwin engages the viewers and the viewers become a part of the art, becoming conscious of themselves within the piece, conscious of their own consciousness, and experiencing the art and their responses to it. Irwin's art emanates a certain energy, which expands our con-

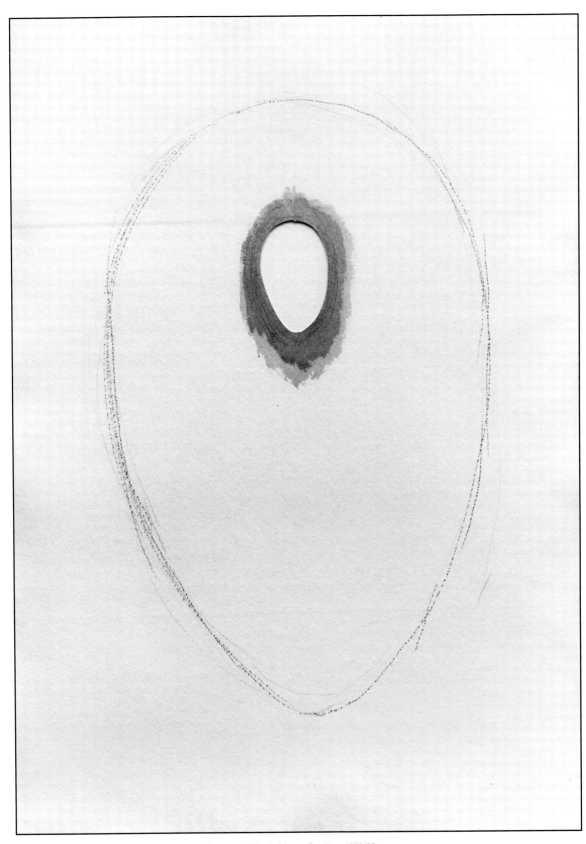

Fig. 31. Christopher Wilmarth, *When Winter on Forgotten Woods Moves Somber* 1979/80
Charcoal and graphite on paper, 31 x 22 3/8"
Private Collection

sciousness and heightens our sensory awareness. This can be seen in his cast wire piece where the line seems to disappear into the wall, drawing us in to it and everything on that wall.


Eric Orr is interested not in Zen but in the Buddhism that existed before the image of the Buddha. "Early Buddhism didn't have the figure...They just worshipped empty space."[36] What is worshipped, he explains, is not the stupa itself but the interior of the form. Zen cannot be understood through intellectual means; it must be experienced. During a trip to Burma, Orr encountered Theravadian Buddhism, in which the emphasis is on empty space; He is concerned with the incorporation into one's own being of "infinite empty space."[37]

In an effort to create an art that was "invisible," Orr built *Zero Mass*. Commissioned by Count Panza di Biumo and shown in 1974 at the Cirrus Gallery in Los Angeles, it is an oval room of seamless white backdrop paper. Lit from outside, the viewer enters from a dark space. Orr stated, "I like to hunt the Void. I have used silence, emptiness and night vision to apprehend my undifferentiated friend..."[38] He creates a space beyond boundaries. For Orr, space is active and the object is passive. He noted that "what I really want is that when you enter that space you're completely changed — you experience ecstasy or something..."[39] It is Nothingness, but a Nothingness that is part of our essential self. The Nothingness which was sought is something that evokes not loneliness or despair or isolation in Buddhism, but contemplation. It is like the hub of a wheel embodying all the force, energy and power–it defines the Nothingness, *Mu,* as in nature, but *Mu* is formless. It is the gaps and intervals between thoughts; that is reality. "In order to be awake to the mind of *Mu*, that is to Reality, we must first give up our attachment to the conscious."[40] In *Zero Mass*, the eyes of the viewer/participant have to adjust to the darkness of the room. At first nothing is visible; gradually the individual begins to discern that there are other figures present, yet the viewer cannot tell the room's size. When one person leaves the space, the people left inside feel as if someone has vanished and sense the loss of presence. One participant stated that "the experience was extremely interesting, both sensuous and enveloping, somewhat like a return to the womb."[41] At first the viewer/participant feels a slight sense of anxiety — being in a dark space with strangers is not the usual museum experience! As the eyes adjust, the viewer comes out of what Orr describes as an "inky" darkness to realize that there are other people in the space. First the visitor sees a shadow and then a form, but visibility stops short of seeing a recognizable face. A person who walks away seems to disappear. The piece brings us back to our primitive or raw vision, night vision without colors, and only shadows remain. Orr considers *Zero Mass* to be one of his most successful pieces. He noted that "it envelops your mind and wipes out where you are."[42] It is

like the mirror in Zen — you can wipe it clean but never remove its reflections.

Orr eliminates both the object and the viewer so that only a shadow for contemplation remains. He forces us to experience the art from within ourselves; to perceive it is to participate in creating the art work. It exists as art only as we exist within it. *Zero Mass* is a koan, a question that can be answered only through the experience of time and space. He has created an environment in which to perceive the totality of the universe. In other works, Orr balances the primal elements of light and space, of fire and water, water and stone. He forces us to dissolve spatial boundaries, to penetrate into a zone where solid forms dissolve and empty... in a recent interview, "...sense of Void into an...

In a later work, Orr creates a calming piece that evokes contemplation because it is meaningless. Water gently flows over a carved foot column on pieces of slate (Fig.62)... to create a form, and the s... water. The water appears to flow up and down simultaneously, always moving, never stagnant (stagnation is death). Orr provides the viewer with proof of the Zen adage that the force of water is stronger than that of stone. It is the Uncarved Block, *Pu,* that denotes the natural state of being, simplicity, purity and infinite potentiality. But it is also an example of *wu-wei*; "Water is of all things most yielding and can overwhelm (rock) which is of all things most hard."[44] It is the sublime force of water. It is Being and Nothingness. Art is now redefined as a natural experience, reminiscent of watching the ocean or a waterfall. "I think art's going to grow up eventually and we're not going to have so much of this dealing with special objects," Orr has said, "It'll be more like an appreciation of what's here...I think it...will eventually get to the way you look at things themselves..."[45]

Does transient afternoon light on the wall look better than art? Orr believes it does: "Every day I open up the shades and the light coming in on the wall — That's it."[46] "The future of art depends on artists not copying art, but finding it."[47] If art is the *Way of Experiencing* rather than the type of object experienced, then the artist's quest is not to create art objects but to direct us to experiences.


"For years," Christopher Wilmarth said, "I have been concerned with the complex problem of implying human presence in non-objective art. The concept of the self-generated form approaches a solution in that the sculpture attains a living presence...These are the places I speak of when I say my sculptures are places to generate experience."[48] Wilmarth's art is also based on the mystical implications of light and the essence of human presence. He portrays in glass and bronze, or watercolor and graphite, the psychic images of *Nothingness* that is the basis of Asian philosophy and that his progenitors, Stéphane Mallarmé, spoke of in his poetry, and Constantin Brancusi captured in his sculptures. Like them, Wilmarth, sought to express, in his forms, the basic concepts of duality and their merger into a unified whole — the epitome of Nothingness.

In several discussions with this author, in 1981 and 1982, Wilmarth pointed out his interest in Eastern philosophy and noted that the idea of *Nothingness* was a critical component in his art. He has also repeatedly reaffirmed his profound respect for Brancusi. The simplicity, refined craftsmanship and spiritual content of the earlier master's work had a profound impact on Wilmarth's work.

Brancusi's interest in Eastern religions and philosophy, Zen Buddhism, and Tibetan Lamaism is well documented. The Tibetan thinker and poet monk Milarepa, was a source for Brancusi's ideas of purity, absoluteness of form, and deliverance from physical weight. Brancusi and Mallarmé ideas confirmed Wilmarth's philosophical outlook.

From 1979 to 1983, Wilmarth created blown glass sculptures, drawings and watercolors, as illustrations for Mallarmé's poems (Figs.31, 79, 80). These are the artist's expressions of Asian philosophy. As Mallarmé sought to describe not objects themselves but their essence, Wilmarth tried to capture in ovoids of translucent glass the Nothingness that Asian philosophers describe. Wilmarth echoed Mallarmé's spirituality in an organic form that is at once a head, the soul, a womb or an egg of light and shadow, the transparent and the opaque. The shapes are reminiscent of Brancusi. Made of blown glass, they represent life, air blown into inanimate material, forced in to expand and embody the breath, the life force, the energy or "*chi.*" The title of the suite is *Breath*, and each work is titled after the first line of a Mallarmé poem. *When Winter on Forgotten Woods Moves Somber* is the first of the suite. In a glass sculpture and drawing the oval or vessel, pale and irregular, is cut into by a smaller irregular oval (Figs. 23, 31). It is the Nothingness from which all subsequent images will arise. *My Old Books Closed* (Fig.79) reveals two contrasting forms merging. In the drawings, pastels, and sculptures the floating amorphous fragile form is contrasted with steel plates or sharp lines.

Wilmarth wrote:

> I'd be driven to leave my studio at the end of the day when the light was just going out. I loved that long light. Then I'd walk across Spring Street and the light would be streaming down, and I'd try to get the last light and the sunset on the Hudson River. I'd go through this ritual several times a week.[49]

A dialogue in which two materials or shapes engage (steel with its ruggedness and permanence, glass with its transparency and vulnerability, or ovals versus lines) transform his art into a balanced and unified whole. Wilmarth uses the glass as a "vehicle" to generate an experience of light.

"My sculptures," he has stated, "are places to generate this experience compressed into light and shadow and return them to the world as a physical poem."[50] Wilmarth wrote the following poem:

> I keep the shades down in the day
> The sun is just a square on the wall
> Every day that square moves down
> across the bed and out into the hall
> just outside a dream will call my name
> and tomorrow's in my room again today.

With glass and steel, Wilmarth created an experience of light — a momentary flash of opposites balanced on a wall. The shadows of light and dark, through translucent glass and steel, create a union of real and ideal, Being and Non-Being. Through the art of our recent generation, Zen teaches that, "Reality is beauty itself; it is the essential self. Beauty reveals itself when the outside and the inside, the subject and the object, become one with the essential self."[51]

# Conclusion

We can now turn off the bright lights of Western criticism and see the transparent thread that runs through contemporary art. The art is a mirror reflecting the ideas of East Asia while also revealing indigenous Western roots, the backdrop upon which Eastern philosophical ideas have been imposed. The art articulates the fact that, beginning with the Zen boom of the 1950s and Jack Kerouac's Beat Generation, there was a renewed but eclectic spiritual atmosphere. The artists who began to experiment in the 1950s influenced the artists of the 1970s. In a period of disillusionment with Western culture, new ideas were easily accepted, and Eastern spirituality affected all aspects of American culture. The sphere of influence and the understanding of it had come a long way since the days of Commodore Perry's first trip to Japan in the mid-19th century. Artists were receptive to new ideas and made Far Eastern philosophy an integral part of their work. Robert Morris, in 1975, summarized the art of his era in the following words:

> The art of the [early] 60's was by and large, open and had an impulse for public scale. It was informed by a logic in its structure, sustained by faith in the significance of abstract art and a belief in a historical unfolding of formal modes which was very close to a belief in progress. The art of that decade was one of dialogue...Mid-way into the 70's...the private replaces the public impulse. Space itself has come to have another meaning. Before it was centrifugal and tough, capable of absorbing monumental impulses. Today it is centripetal and intimate, demanding demarcation and enclosure. Deeply skeptical of experience beyond the reach of the body, the more formal aspect of the work in question provides a place in which the perceiving self might take measure of certain aspects of our own physical existence. Equally skeptical of participating in any public enterprise, its other side

The art created by many artists in the last twenty-five years points the mind... and to perceive one's own being as a microcosm in the universe. Zen, and the art that it inspired, forces the mind to move beyond surface forms. The art must be internalized. It depends as much on the perception of the viewer/participant as it does on its own inherent qualities. Through a limited, controlled format, Patricia Johanson, Michelle Stuart, Eric Orr, Robert Irwin and Michael Singer have created an image of the totality of the universe. The works of these artists direct the viewer to the microcosm which represents the macrocosm. Artists such as Carl Andre, Walter DeMaria, Robert Morris, Christopher Wilmarth and Richard Serra structure the Void to evoke contemplation of the Totality of the universe. Their art plays with perception and reminds the viewer that there is more to reality, that ultimately we must transcend our senses; the art is there as a guide. Our mind internalizes the art and we pass "from the perception of discrete phenomena, of objects...to the conception of invisible agent manipulating these objects." [53] The art points us to life's experiences; to the Center of Experience.

The art works become the koan, the unanswerable question that can be answered only through experience. The answer is intuitive rather than a logical rationalization. Herrigel has written, "If you want to understand Zen, understand it right away without deliberation, with-out turning your head this way or that. For while you are doing this, the object you have been seeking is no longer there." [54] Like Zen, this art seeks to restore the participant to the experience of original inseparability, to return to the original state of purity and transparency.

The artists discussed here are only a sampling of those who are aware of Asian philosophical thought and who have experimented with perception. Many works created since the mid-1950s are about process, change, and nature in ways that expand and exemplify concepts of Asian philosophy. They represent an experimental art which evokes a contemplative and inward response. While these artists may also have been reading Merleau-Ponty or other philosophers, one does not preclude the other. In discussing Zen or Taoism with these artists, it becomes clear that there was an awareness of Asian philosophical ideas in contemporary art and society. They were part of an environment that cultivated these ideas in their art. Few know it or understand it as a Zen scholar might, few understand its full ramifications, but what is irrefutable is the way in which they have "inhaled" these ideas, and infused their art with the essence of Asian philosophical thought. What is most significant is that at a point in time in our recent history, artists have turned to alternative ideas in order to create an experiential milieu that would help us to better perceive and understand our world. The artists have embodied some of the Eastern *Yin* and combined it with the Western *Yang* to try to create an art that points the way to understanding the Tao in art.

# Notes

1. Smithson was introduced to Zen through the Beat poets, Sol LeWitt has also noted his affinity to Eastern philosophy. The connections of these artists to Zen is the source of a future study.

2. Geri De Paoli, interview with the artists, quoted in "Meditations and Humor", *The Transparent Thread*.

3. Coosje Van Bruggen, "Entrance, Entrapment, Exit", *Artforum*, 24 (Summer 1986), p. 88.

4. Cage has stated that when he needed a teacher one appeared. Interview with author, Dec.1989

5. Brecht was also influenced by Eastern philosophy.

6. Terry Miller, *Images of Change*, NY: E.P. Dutton & Co., 1976.

7. Frederick Wilkinson, *Swords and Daggers,* NY: Hawthorne books, 1967, See pp. 50, 54 quoted in Robert Morris "Present Tense of Space," 1978.

8. Robert Morris, "Some Notes on the Phenomenology of Making: The Search for the Motivated," *Artforum* (April 1970), p. 66.

9. Robert Morris, "Aligned with Nazca." *Artforum* Vol. 14, Oct. 1975.

10. Robert Morris, "American Artist," *Art in America*, Dec. 1981, p. 104.

11. Quoted in Diane Waldman, *Singer*, NY: Guggenheim Museum, 1984, p. 21.

12. Quoted in Waldman, p. 22.

13. Kate Linker "Michael Singer: A Position In, and On, Nature," p. 189.

14. Donald Kuspit, "Michael Singer at Sperone Westwater Fischer," *Art In America* Vol 64, July-Aug. 1976, p. 105.

15. Interview between Singer and Gelburd, Summer 1989.

16. Diane Waldman, *Singer*, Guggenheim Museum, 1984.

17. Ralph Waldo Emerson, *Selected Prose and Poetry*.

18. Michelle Stuart wears a ring that opens and closes and is a lotus!

19. Interview by Gail Gelburd with Michelle Stuart, Summer 1989.

20. Tom Sandquist, Michelle Stuart: Voyages (Hillwood Gallery, C.W. Post), 1985.

21. Robert Hobbs, Michelle Stuart, exhibition catalog, n.d..

22. D.T. Suzuki, *Zen and Japanese Culture*, p. 361.

23. From a letter to Gail Gelburd from Patricia Johanson, March 20, 1986.

24. Quoted in David H. Engel, *Japanese Gardens For Today*. (Vermont: Tuttle Co., 1959), p. 13.

25. Warner, p. 105.

26. Correspondence between Gail Gelburd and Patricia Johanson, March, 1987, in which the artist refers to a passage in the introduction by Raymond Blankney for *The Way of Life* by Lao Tzu, 4th printing 1959, New American Library, p. 42-43.

27. Elenor Munro, *Originals: American Woman Artists*, (NY: 1979), p. 46.

28. From lecture given September 10, 1986, Dallas, Texas by Patricia Johanson, unpublished manuscript.

29. Interview 6/19/86 between Gail Gelburd and Patricia Johanson.

30. Correspondence between Gail Gelburd and Patricia Johanson, March 1987.

31. Lucy Lippard "Stemming From...", Patricia Johanson: Fair Park Lagoon, Dallas and Color Gardens, Rosa Esman Gallery, March 15 - April 9, 1983, p. 12.

32. Weschler, *Seeing is Forgetting the Name of the Thing One Sees*. (Berkeley: University of California Press) 1982.

33. Weschler.

34. Weschler, p. 17.

35. Weschler, p. 59.

36. Typed manuscript of tape recorded conversation between Eric Orr, Ron Cooper and Larry Bell Teo, New Mexico, January 3, 1983. Repeated in interview with Gail Gelburd, December 20, 1989.

37. Interview between Eric Orr and Gail Gelburd, Dec. 20, 1989.

38. Statement prepared for 1982 Documenta by Eric Orr.

39. Thomas McEvilley "Negative Presences in Secret Spaces: The Art of Eric Orr" *Artforum* 20 (Summer 1982), p. 58-66.

40. D.T. Suzuki, *Zen and Japanese Culture*, (N.J.: Princeton University Press, 1973), p. 360.

41. Janet Kutner, "Los Angeles in the 70's", *Art News* 76 (Dec. 1977), p. 104.

42. Interview with Eric Orr, Dec. 20, 1989.

43. Ibid.

44. *Tao Te Ching*, Chapter, 43, p. 21.

45. Thomas McEvilley "Journeys In and Out of the Body: Proto Materialism, Eric Orr," *Images and Issues*, Spring 1981, p. 18.

46. Interview with Eric Orr by Gail Gelburd on Dec. 20, 1989.

47. Statement prepared for 1982 Documenta by Eric Orr.

48. Statement by Wilmarth September 1974, printed in Museum of Modern Art, *Christopher Wilmarth*, N.Y., 1989, p. 14.

49. Maurice Poirier, "Christopher Wilmarth: The Medium is Light," *Art News* (84:Dec. 1985), pp. 68-75.

50. *Wilmarth: Nine Clearings for a Standing Man* (Hartford: Wadsworth Athenaeum 1974).

51. Shoei Ando, *Zen and American Transcendentalism*. (Tokyo: Hokuseido Press, 1970), p. 30.

52. Robert Morris, "Aligned with Nazca" *Artforum*, Vol. 14, Oct. 1975, p. 39.

53. Herbert Read, *Icon and Idea*. (New York: Schoker Books, 1965, p. 54.

54. Eugen Herrigel, *Zen and the Art of Archery*. New York, 1957.

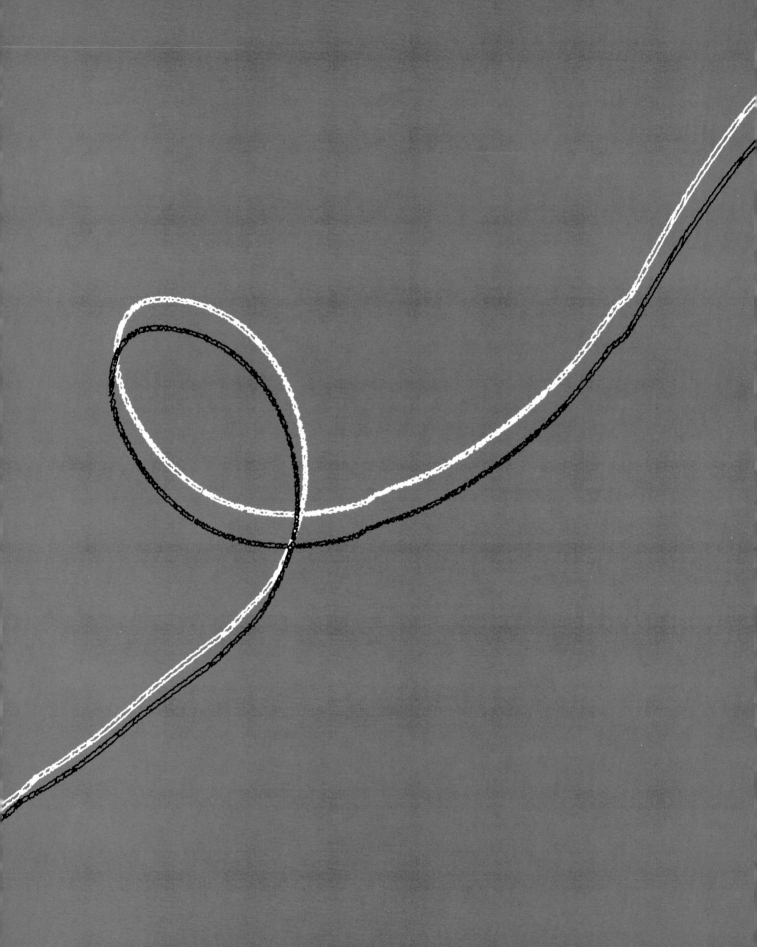

# Artists Section

# Carl Andre

Andre's sculpture, serenely ordered, presents a quiet, austere world. Born in the shipbuilding town of Quincy, Massachusetts, Andre was the youngest of three children. His father was a marine draftsman and a skilled woodcarver. The wooden girders and steel beams in the town's shipyards and the uncarved blocks in its abandoned quarries became ingrained in his memory, and years later found expression in his art.

Andre studied with Patrick Morgan at the Phillips Academy in Andover, Massachusetts from 1951-53 with Frank Stella and Hollis Frampton (the filmmaker). After working briefly for the Boston Gear Works he went to England and France. He spent two years as an intelligence analyst with the U.S. Army in North Carolina. In 1957 he moved to New York City and worked as an editorial assistant for a publisher of textbooks. Frampton and Andre had a mutual interest in poetry. In 1958 Andre spent most of his time working on poetry and occasional drawings. That summer he began making some paintings and sculptures. Frampton states, Andre "...worked wherever he happened to be, with what was at hand. His studio was his mind, so to speak. Anyone who admired a piece was welcome to shelter it, and a few did, but nothing encumbered him for too long. When he moved, the work was left behind."[1]

Andre's early work had a direct connection with the art of Brancusi. Profoundly influenced by Eastern philosophies, Brancusi had found in them not only an inspiration, but also guidance for both his art and his existence. Inspired by Brancusi's *Endless Column*, Andre explains the importance of Brancusi's work for him.

> Brancusi to me, is the greatest link into the earth—. They (sculptures) reach up and they drive down into the earth with a kind of verticality which is not terminal: the top of the head and the bottom of the feet were the limits of the sculpture. Brancusi's sculpture continued beyond its vertical limit and beyond its many found materials, not that that's important. But he used and combined these particles with those particles that were heterogeneous (not homogeneous.) He definitely did combine particles in building up these pedestals which

was, for me, the greatest interest in his work— that those pedestals were the culmination of the materials.[2]

During 1958, Andre made several small sculptures, in plexiglas and wood, which were drilled and incised rather than carved or modelled. The mark on the block was minimal, the shapes were primary forms. Andre stated, "Up to a certain time I was cutting into things. Then I realized that the thing I was cutting was the cut. Rather than cut into the material, I now use the material as the cut in space."[3] This is his manifestation of *Pu*, Andre has admitted to this interest in correspondance with the author.[4]

Andre's employment as a freight brakeman and conductor for the Pennsylvania Railroad in the early 1960s made a lasting effect on him. Impressed by the seemingly eternal extension of the railroad tracks, Andre developed a new aspect of his art—horizontality. "All I'm doing," the artist said, "is putting Brancusi's 'Endless Column' on the ground instead of in the sky." His floor pieces, articulate and earthbound, geometric and symmetrical, horizontal in design with repetitive order, embody the concept of balance. It is the manifestation of Tai Chi.

His work as an artist has consisted of selecting and arranging things. In terms of the Minimalist quality of Andre's work "One could say that Andre has given up everything and yet he has given up nothing...Andre's art is free...to dwell upon the fundamental sources of reality."[5] Taoist concepts of contemplation and intuition have had a significant influence on Carl Andre. As in Oriental philosophy, it meant a cleansing of one's spirit and a claiming of the inner being.

1 Hollis Frampton, "letter to Enno Develing" in *Carl Andre,* exhibition catalogue, Haag Gemeentemuseum, August 23-October 5, 1969, p.8.
2 "An Interview with Carl Andre", *Artforum* vii/10 June 1970, p.61. Interview with Phyllis Tuchman.
3 David Bourdon "The Razed Sites of Carl Andre: A Sculptore Laid Low by the Brancusi Syndrome", v/2 October 1966, p.15.
4 Answers to questionaire sent to Gelburd in 1985.
5 Waldman, *Carl Andre,* Guggenheim Museum, p.21.

Fig. 32. Carl Andre, *Concrete Crib* 1965
Cast concrete bars
14 unit stack, 7 tiers of 2 bars each
Courtesy Rose Art Museum, Brandeis University,
Waltham, Massachusetts, Anonymous Gift

67

# Robert Arneson

Fifty-nine-year-old Robert Arneson, ceramic sculptor and accomplished draftsman, graduated from the California College of Arts and Crafts in Oakland in 1954. He has been an influential professor at the University of California, Davis, since1962, where he was recently awarded that institution's distinguished faculty medal.

While teaching in a high school he became aware of the possibilities for artistic expression in the medium of ceramics through the art of Peter Vol kous. Vol kous' work in turn led to Arneson's reading of Bernard Leach, through which he was first exposed to Asian thought.

After some years of making works in the spirit of Japanese tea ceremony vessels, Arneson's work, the making of a clay beer bottle (1961), *Six-Pack* (Fig.35) signaled a new direction. During the 1960s he assisted in the birth of Funk Art with the creation of the ceramic sculpture, *Funk John*, in 1963 (later destroyed). His unique ceramic sculpture, consisting of household objects, food, plumbing equipment, and portrait heads in unusual juxtapositions, has been labled Pop, Funk, Expressionist and has been instrumental in changing art establishment notions about clay as a fine art medium.

The term Funk originated in jazz. It meant something that was so unconventional, so bad, it was good. The magic of Funk can be likened to jazz and can be compared to the phenomenon of the yin-yang. The magic is found in the mystery of the balance, the tension, it's in the "space between," what you cannot see or measure. Arneson speaks of jazz in discussing Asian thought in connection with openness and the trust in chance operations.

In a conversation about Asian thought and American art, Arneson tells of becoming receptive to ideas from the East. In the following interview his discussion of a short-hand use of the *I-Ching* and his ideas on humor speak eloquently about the Americanization of elements of the Asian world view.

From an interview with Robert Arneson by Geri DePaoli

When did I become interested in Eastern thought? It had to have come along after art school (1950-54). It was when I became interested in ceramics, because, one has to look to the East in terms of pottery. American pottery at that time was inspired by a Calvinist attitude of usefulness. Products tended to be utilitarian, cold and without a philosophical presence. You could say they were industrial. If you are seriously interested, you look, and do some reading. The readings I would have done would have been Bernard Leach, "The Art of the Potter". The book really traces his transformation, an Englishman going to Japan to teach English and watercolor. The idea of imposing the imperial attitude on Eastern thought. It was the experience of seeing that idea, in Leach, of imperial thought undergoing transformation, a whole sense of being, and coming back a potter....a very inspiring book...
"There is an opening in jazz..that in my mind is equivalent to Eastern thought. It transcends...it requires giving up structure and taking on understanding of the person who's playing with you. You have the sense that it's an interior thing...
...Alan Watts had a radio program in the 60's . It's still going, the recordings, and I still listen at 4:30. Now I listen in the most proper way, background noise, but of course you still listen.
I came to a lot of this also by just hanging out, listening to others, I never programmed myself; just hunching along. In discussing our works, between artists, I acquired alot second hand. It was good enough that I didn't have to trust the 'ivory tower.'
There was a kind of Americanization of these ideas, the important things, the centeredness is humor, it is also in the cartoon, that allows the natural flow. Square one to square four, four square. That is American...those are our teachers. The idea was to get the line. Those cartoons mean alot to me, they taught me to draw. It is in much the same manner that a Chinese painter of the 16th century would have to go out and make copies of past masters in order to emulate. If you look closely, it is the closest thing to Eastern writing, certainly calligraphy, that we have.
Yes, and humor....you certainly see it in John Cage.... He is, in my mind, one of the greatest humorists. Unfortunately, you just don't get any of it through a tape. When he was at Davis and doing those performances at Freeborn Hall...that was it...uncorking the champagne bottle...he had the timing of Jack Benny.
He taught a class using the I-Ching. The students would select a number, it would refer to a page in the text and that was their assignment. I've explored the I-Ching attitude of 'just do it', it's a short-hand method I use. I 've done it in class, assignments drawn randomly from the Sears catalog.
In the West, humor is a problem. It's been since Greek times, people take it personally. Have you read that book, The Closing of the American Mind ? ... it's very narrow. There is room for only one kind of thought, Western thought. It is not true, there's another people out there, and they have created another philosophy..it might even be better than ours!

Fig. 33. Robert Arneson *The Gift* 1962
Collage
18 3/4 x 14"
Collection, Rene and Veronica di Rosa

Fig. 34. Robert Arneson, *Heart Box* 1965
Ceramic sculpture, contains 6 small hearts
9 1/2 x 9 x 8"
Jedermann Collection, N. A.

Fig. 35. Robert Arneson, *Six-pack* 1964
Ceramic sculpture
10 x 9 1/4 x 6 1/2"
Collection, Rene and Veronica di Rosa

Fig. 26. Robert Arneson, *No Matter* 1974
Collage and mixed media
33 x 25"
Collection, Rene and Veronica di Rosa

Fig. 37. Robert Arneson, *Chinese Proverb* 1969
Ceramic sculpture/celedon glazed procelain
4 x 3 1/2 x 4 1/2"
Courtesy of the Artist

Fig. 38. Robert Arneson, *With Full Force* 1970
Celedon glazed porcelain and stoneware
7 x 9 1/8 x 4 1/2"
Richard L. Nelson Gallery & The Fine Arts Collection,
University of California, Davis, Gift of Roland Petersen

# John Baldessari

John Anthony Baldessari was born in National City, California in 1937. He was interested in art from an early age and was self-motivated. His study of art was at San Diego State College and he has taught at the California Institute for the Arts in Valencia from 1970 until 1987.

Baldessari is an artist with an intellectual bent who once said, "I live in my mind." He had considered attending Princeton Theological Seminary and also thought of being an art critic. He "clearly has a writers sensibility" (note Artnews , January, 1986).

His comments on the influence of Far Eastern philosophy have special importance because of their relevance to his work he transmits his assimilation of the Asian world view by his method of teaching. His students underscore his importance in their development; David Salle refers to him as a "guru." Some of Baldessari's students who have achieved critical acclaim include: Matt Mullican, Ross Bleckner, David Salle, Eric Fischl, Troy Brauntuch, and Jack Goldstein.

Baldessari shares with Arneson, Marisol, Rosenquist and Wiley an interest in cartoons as a special key to the American nature. They also share the use of humor in their work and in their outlook on life; it is a Zen humor. Baldessari, Arneson and Wiley, all teachers, use humor to alter the perspective of their students. Some of the students, however, are not aware of the Far Eastern origin of some of their teachers' attitudes and practices but some do discover the source and have pursued a study and use of Asian thought.

From an interview with John Baldessari by Geri DePaoli:

> I suppose I first came into real contact with Asian ideas through the general dissemination by the Beat movement in California, especially in San Francisco and through Alan Watts. I still keep a copy of *The Wisdom of Insecurity* (Watts). I read Suzuki and *Zen and the Art of Archery* early. Later the ideas re-surfaced in *Zen and the Art of Motorcycle Maintenance.*
>
> Also in my early work, and it's still there, John Cage's use of Zen was a pretty strong influence.
>
> One way I remember being influenced by these ideas was in the sense of economy, the sort of "less is more" idea. Also the penchant for paradox which I seemed to identify with.
>
> The idea of non-linear thinking, global thinking

or being able to make what would be identified by the Western mind as non-logical connections. And as you know, all of this is still very prevalent in my work.

The pictograms interest me, something that can be abstract and quite literal; something that would stand for something else. The idea of plainness was fascinating, interest in the mundane which could also be profound.

And like the koan, there is a statement which I will always remember, I wish I had said it but it was Sol Lewitt, "Once you get past boredom, it's interesting." I work on many levels: paradoxic, profound, and banal at the same time there are always many opportunities for connection.

There are indeed different attitudes toward nature between the Orient and the West, like for me Godzilla movies demonstrate Eastern thought. He is an element of nature not an evil monster.

In Oriental art, they're more comfortable with a sense of humor because they can see great profundity in humor. I doubt if it's even labeled humor. I love the outrageous humor, like that quality of the Zen monks. Obviously there's a sort of a redemption in humor. That's one of the things that I really miss in reading the bible; there's no sense of humor in it. No indication in any one place of any humor, which I find amazing.

Asian music has interested me and has been an influence, it is non-structured, at least in the Western sense. There are no highs, peaks, beginning, middles and ends. That has influenced me a lot. It's the sort of leveling , one thing no more important than another, sort of anti-Wagnerian.

The idea of collapsing dualities, process/ product...I'm very little product oriented. It is a fact that I burned all of my paintings. It's the doing that is important. My work I look at as sort of elements in a conversation. I think that when I'm working at my best I can sort of trigger levers in people's minds.

The void in the East is important as it is an inverting of priorities. It shows the different states of perspective. I also use the long horizontal, it's a way of escaping Western space, or composition. It irks me that it's [the vertical format] considered the norm. From the East I got a spare lean way, I tell my students to 'cut out the fat', avoid overloading. I try to get them to find their nature, their strength, and go with it. No one thing is more important than any other, every way has potential. Space is no more and no less important than any object.

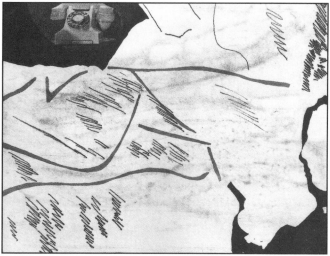
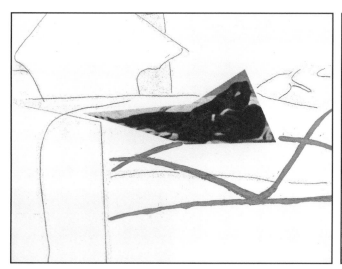

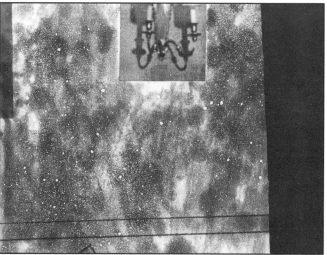

Fig. 39. John Baldessari, *Black Dice* 1982
Color etchings in drypoint, aquatint, sugarlift, soft ground,
photoetching and black and white photograph
16 1/2 x 19 3/4" each
Courtesy Peter Blum Editions, New York

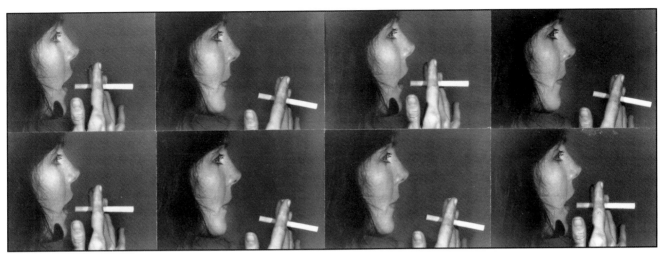

Fig. 40. John Baldessari, *Binary Code Series: Woman with Cigarette Yes No Yes No*
*Yes No No Yes* 1974
Black and white photographs
18 3/4 x 55"
Courtesy Sonnabend Gallery

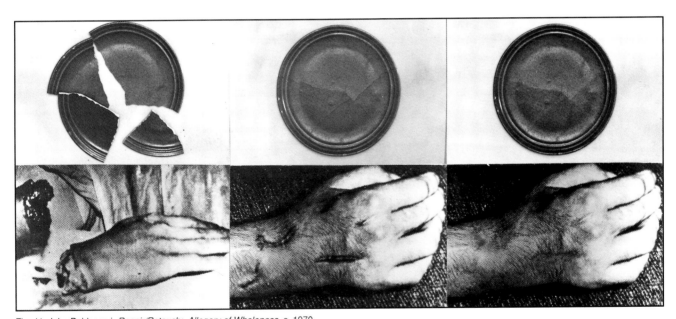

Fig. 41. John Baldessari, *Repair/Retouch: Allegory of Wholeness* c. 1970
Photo collage and mixed media
16 x 20"
Jedermann Collection, N. A.

# Walter De Maria

Walter De Maria was born in 1935 in Albany, California, and attended the University of California at Berkeley from 1953 to 1959, receiving a Bachelor of Arts degree in history and a Master of Arts degree in art. DeMaria's first interest was music and he began, early in his career, to incorporate Asian concepts of chance and randomness. He worked with LaMonte Young, a musician profoundly influenced by Eastern philosphy and paid homage to John Cage with his construction titled *Statue for John Cage.* A work of DeMaria's which explicates his interest in chance and randomness is titled *360° I-Ching.* The photograph of this piece was personally lent to this exhibition with full knowledge of the theme. In 1960, he moved to New York and began creating works of art, such as *Boxes for Meaningless Work,* using unpainted plywood. The influence of Zen through the sages of his era, such as John Cage, began to be noticeable in his penciling of words such as "Water, Water, Water."

While many artists were beginning to travel west, (Heizer was creating *Double Negative* (1969-1971), Oppenheim's *Branded Hillside* was done in 1969, and Smithson completed his *Spiral Jetty* in 1970, in the West). De Maria began to utilize the geometric hard-edge style of Minimalism, to evoke gestural qualities associated with the Abstract Expressionists using the earth as the medium. De Maria was gently marking the earth. He produced his first Western work in April of 1968: two parallel lines, a mile long, laid down in chalk on the Mojave desert in California. *Mile Long Drawing* is the only reference point in space.

On November 1, 1977, De Maria's monumental environmental sculpture, *The Lightning Field,* was completed in its present physical form. Commissioned and maintained by the Dia Foundation, the *Lightning Field* is a rectangular grid which measures 5,280 feet (one mile) by 3,300 feet (about one kilometer). It contains 400 highly polished stainless-steel poles with pointed tips, spaced 220 feet apart. The 400 poles measure two inches in diameter and averages 20 feet, 7 1/2 inches in height. They are in twenty-five rows of sixteen poles in each row. The visitor/participant to the site stays for at least 24 hours and watches nature change, reflected in the poles. The art becomes the experience. The work of De Maria propels the viewer/participant inward and beyond their external form. He prefers unified, meditative, and elevated forms. Simplification and unity are the keys to his vision. His art work in polished stainless steel, shiny and fluidic, mirrors the world around it and fluctuates by virtue of the changes of light; it heightens the realm of contemplation. In his works, idea and image, form and thought, are one.

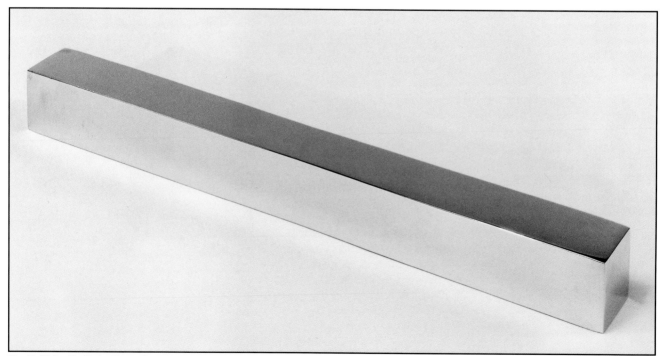

Fig. 42. Walter De Maria, *Energy Bar* 1966
Stainless steel
1 1/2 x 1 1/2 x 14 1/2"
Courtesy Vassar College Art Gallery, Poughkeepsie, New York
Gift of Mr. and Mrs. Frederic Ossorio  77.60.5

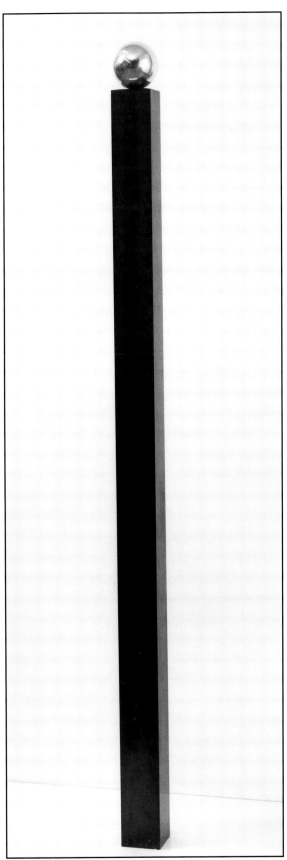

Fig. 43. Walter De Maria, *Bronze Column* 1966
Bronze and stainless steel
54 x 3 x 3"
The Whitney Museum of American Art, New York
Gift of Howard and Jean Lipman  78.79

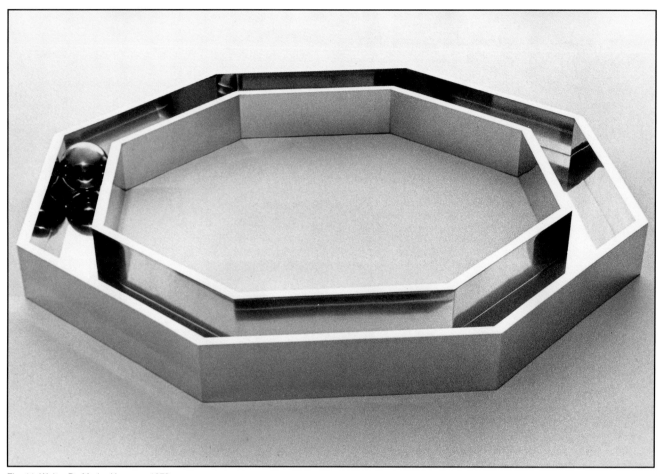

Fig. 44. Walter De Maria, *Hexagon* 1973
Stainless steel
3 5/8 x 42 x 36 1/2"
Courtesy The Rivendell Collection

# Robert Irwin

Robert Irwin began as an Abstract Expressionist in the 1960s and then gradually pared down, eliminating frame, object, and imagery. In 1970, he eliminated his studio altogether. His experience and interest in alternative states of consciousness and alternative philosophies can be traced to events and contacts early in his career.

During the late 1940s, Irwin was heading south from Paris toward Morocco. While passing through Barcelona, he heard about Ibiza, a small island off the coast of Spain. He went to this quiet, peaceful, dry, and barren island, rented a small cabin and then avoided speaking with anyone for eight months. He recalled how it felt to eliminate oneself from the everyday world as we know it.

> Well, what was happening to me as I was on my way to Ibiza was that I was pulling all those plugs out, one at a time: books, language, social contacts. And what happens at a certain point as you get down to the last plugs, its like the Zen thing of having no ego: it becomes scary, its like maybe you're going to lose yourself. And boredom then becomes extremely painful. You really are bored and alone and vulnerable on the sense of having no outside supports in terms of your own being. But when you get them all pulled out, a little period goes by, and then its absolutely serene, its terrific. It just becomes really pleasant, because you're out, you're all the way out.[1]

From 1957 to 1962, Robert Irwin became involved with a group called Ferus. Although he was creating Abstract Expressionist works successfully in 1957, he was attracted to an exhibit at the nearby Ferus Gallery. Formed by Edward Kienholz and Walter Hopps, this exhibit, "Objects on the New Landscape Demanding of the Eye," included works by Richard Diebenkorn, Frank Lobdell, and Clyford Still, artists who were united by their common hostility to other Los Angeles art galleries. When Irving Blum took over the Ferus Gallery in 1958 he added Irwin. The new Ferus core included Altoon, Bengston, Kauffman, Moses, Kienholz, Ken Price, and John Mason. "Ferus was like a magnet," Irwin later said of this group. It was an energy level, a level of conviction, an attitude about art, a general attitude about the significance of the work, a sense that we were all at the right place at just the right time."[2]

Irwin and his Ferus friends dabbled in Zen and other Oriental philosophies. "None of the people I knew really read," he said, "and I didn't either. That doesn't mean that I didn't skim. For example, I remember a book of haiku making the rounds, and I may have read two or three of them without really focusing."[3]

His associates, Craig Kauffman and Allen Lynch were especially interested in Oriental philosophy. Lynch had a large collection of Raku. Irwin stated, "Those hand-held paintings got very quote Zen-like in a meditative sense, as opposed to an open gestural sense... And the fact that you were meant to hold them meant that they could only be experienced privately, intimately."[4] At this point Irwin began to look for another mode, he eliminated the object and concentrated on light and space.

1 Weschler, Lawrence. *Seeing is Forgetting the Name of the Thing One Sees: A Life of Contemporary Artist Robert Irwin.* University of California Press, Berkeley, and Los Angeles, California, 1982, p. 36-7.

2 Weschler, p. 47.
3 Weschler, p. 37-8.
4 Weschler, p. 38.

# Patricia Johanson

Patricia Johanson remembers Ise, Kokadera, Stonehenge, Nazca, Midwestern Indian mounds, Mayan ruins and Angkor Wat. She admits to creating art within a historical context and to an affinity with Eastern philosophical ideas.[1] Johanson has studied with and befriended many artists who, like her, sought to divest themselves of the traditional object in art and to embrace the philosophical tenets of the Far East. At Bennington College, she studied with Tony Smith and worked in Frederick Kiesler's studio. Later, she studied at the Art Students League and met Barnett Newman. When she enrolled for a master's degree at Hunter College she not only studied with Tony Smith again, but she also attended Ad Reinhardt's Oriental art course and was a classmate of Robert Morris. She admires Noguchi's sense of the spirituality in nature. Each of these mentors were also interested in eastern philosophy.

In 1966, Johanson traveled to Texas and New Mexico, where she catalogued paintings, photographs and newspaper clippings for Georgia O'Keeffe. An ardent admirer of O'Keeffe, Johanson recalls that O'Keeffe had read and discussed with her the writings of Fenollosa, Lafcadio Hearne, and Arthur Wesley Dow, and the theories of "Notan" (shadows) while they were together in Abiquiu.[2] "I think I'm the person I am today," she has since said, "because of knowing her."[3] Johanson is also familiar with the work of the other artists inspired by the Far East, including Mark Tobey, Morris Graves and John Cage, and she shows an indebtedness to Frank Lloyd Wright, the architect, who was profoundly influenced by Oriental aesthetics. Her *Swan Orchid House* (1974) might be compared to Wright's architecture "Trirranna" (1956-58) in New Canaan, Connecticut, that they share in eccentric spans of curvilinear organic forms that confound indoor and outdoor spaces.

In 1982, Johanson visited Japan and participated in religious ceremonies at Kokadera Temple. She visited Japanese gardens, read Haiku poetry, wrote the sutras, has been to the Chinese opera, and taken Karate. She is aware of Far Eastern culture and envelopes it in an art form that reintegrates man with nature in an everchanging spectrum of infinite forms. She has avidly collected rocks, in order to make her own rock gardens and she has observed the reflections, shadows and the water that changed the personality of the rock.

Trained as a landscape architect, she now creates large scale environmental art projects which use natural elements such as flowers or snakes. Two recent major works are creative solutions for ecology issues: restoration of a lagoon in Dallas and construction of a water purification site in San Francisco. Her works merge art, science, and philosophy in order to bring us closer to our place in the universe.

---

1 From a letter to the author from the artist dated March 20, 1986.
2 Letter dated March 20, 1986.
3 Interview with the artist 6/19/89 in which she recalled these discussions while she was with O'Keeffe in Abiquiu.

Fig. 45. Patricia Johanson, *Pompeys Pillar* 1964
Acrylic
80 x 80 x 2"
Courtesy the Artist

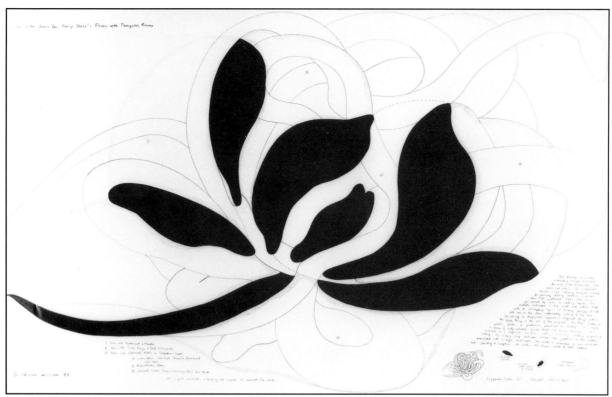

Fig. 46. Patricia Johanson, *Snake in the Grass For Phillip Glass - Flower with Triangular Rooms* 1985
Ink on mylar
42 x 69"
Courtesy the Artist

Fig. 47. Patricia Johanson, *Snake in the Grass For Phillip Glass - Pattern of Water* 1985
Acrylic, ink and gouache on mylar
42 x 69"
Courtesy the Artist

Fig. 48. Patricia Johanson,
*Study for Flower Fountain* 1980
Pen and ink, charcoal on vellum
36 x 51"
The Metropolitan Museum of Art
Purchase, Louis and Bessie Adler Foundation, Inc.
Gift, (Seymour M. Klein, Pres.) 1981

Fig. 49. Patricia Johanson, *Maquette for "Flower Fountain*" 1980
Stoneware and fiberglass
50 x 32 x 7"
The Metropolitan Museum of Art, Gift of the Artist, 1981

Fig. 50. Patricia Johanson, *Maquette for Flower Fountain*
(detail)

# Jasper Johns

Jasper Johns has been closely associated with John Cage and a group of artists who were directly involved with Buddhist and Tao and I-Ching practices and ideas from the 1950s to the present. They all exchanged reading materials, engaged in lively discussions and applied the ideas and practices from Asia in their art and life. Johns traveled to Japan in the 1950s, and has expressed a deep interest in Asian philosophy. Many Asian concepts appear in the titles of recent works of art such as *Usuyuki, Tantric Detail* and *The Seasons*.

*The Seasons* (Figs. 51, 52) are in the format of the four vertical panels representing the four seasons as in Japanese screens and Chinese painting. The iconography of the seasons follows in the tradition of the koan in its presentation of paradoxical imagery.

The repeated marks enlivening the ground of some of Johns' works have been described as crosshatching (*The Seasons*). The random distribution and occasional repetition of groupings of lines can also be compared to the cast straws in the practice of the *I-Ching*. These intersecting marks create a space likened to the Buddhist void out of which forms arise and in turn disappear. There is no separation of form or void, objects exist in conditional relationship.

Shortly after Herrigel's *Zen and the Art of Archery* was published in 1953, and after John's trip to Japan, Johns painted *Target*. The target functions as a ground or focus for meditation, a mandala or diagram of the universe.

When Johns uses ordinary objects such as beer cans, light bulbs (Fig. 53), forks they are presented as a koan is presented. They seem to be readable but they do not refer to themselves nor their function. Their presence cannot be explained by any rational conclusion or logical equation. They hold the potential for transformation.[1]

Johns' aesthetic resembles the Japanese expressions of wabi and sabi (the fleeting beauty, poetic potential of the moment, the richness and power of the patina of time) and the work contains the subtle humor of the koan. The subject of his objects is potential, experience. His work gives no narrative, preaches no conclusion, but seeks to transfer the chi, the life breath or spirit resonance, of objects and of existence.

His statements should be read with a Zen/Tao overlay.

> As well as I can tell, I am concerned with
> space. With some idea about space. And
> then as soon as you break space, then you
> have things
> the idea of background (and background
> music)..idea of neutrality...air and the idea of
> air...(In breathing-in and out)[2]
> Satie's "Furniture Music" now serving as background for music as well as background for
> conversation. Puns on intentions.
> The condition of a presence.
> The condition of being there.
> its own work
> its own
> its
> it
> (quotes reprinted in Jasper Johns: Work Since
> 1974, Mark Rosenthal)
> One need only juxtapose the above statement
> to the Zen notion of "suchness"

Following the interests of the visual artists in the 1950s and 1960s, Johns' work proceeds from concerns with the void (space) to the emergence of "things." It is emblematic of the shifting concepts of space and the realignments of basic notions: ego, void, matter, time, meaning, being. He derives affirmation for his insights and experiences from a long acquaintance with Asian thought as well as from the writings of Wittgenstein whose late works are often compared to Zen, especially in the conception of emptiness.

---

[1] The notion of transformation is different than those generated from a Western philosophical base. Compare the Zen/Tao conception with that discussed in Mashun, Pop Art and the Critics.

[2] The Chinese *chi*, life-breath, spirit resonance, was a common term from books on Chinese painting and was used liberally. The use of the term "breath" by a number of artists is meant in the manner of the chi.

Figs. 51,52. Jasper Johns, *The Seasons* 1977
Etching/aquatint
20 3/8 x 12 1/2" each, from set of four
Los Angeles County Museum of Art,
General Acquisition Fund
Graphic Art Council (m.88.77.a-d)

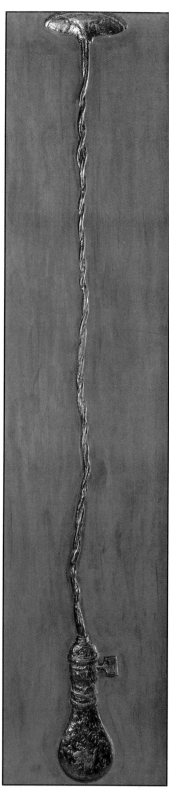

Fig. 53. Jasper Johns, *Light Bulb* 1968
Wax and acrylic on masonite
37 1/2 x 8 1/4"
Los Angeles County Museum of Art,
Gift of Jasper Johns (m.69.77.211)

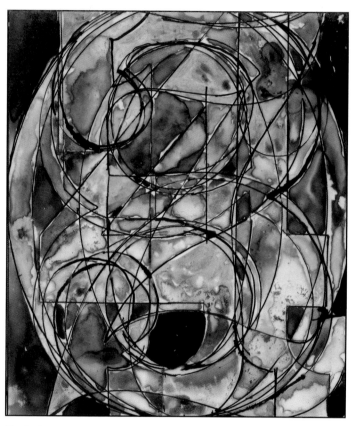

Fig. 54. Jasper Johns, *O through 9* 1979
Ink on plastic
11 7/8 x 10 3/4"
Collection of Margo Leavin

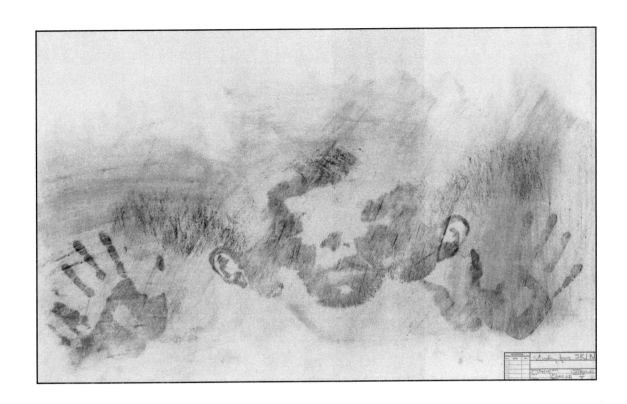

Figs. 55,56. Jasper Johns, *Study for Skin* 1962
Charcoal on paper
22 x 34" ea.
Collection of the Artist

# Escobar Marisol

Marisol studied with Hans Hoffman in the 1950s and from her teacher's ideas about push/pull, she has developed her interest in form/void relationships and the tension of two- and three-dimensional space. Her formation as an artist in the 1950s and 1960s included a shared philosophical environment with artists in New York, San Francisco and Chicago. The artist's world then was permeated by an air filled with Zen/Tao, I Ching, Existential and Marxist notions. Ideas about space, time, form, void, and the nature of matter were common topics of discussion at gatherings of artists. She has stated that the Asian world view has been a most important element in the formation of her personal philosophy and in her work.[1]

Although Marisol is always listed among Pop artists, Lucy Lippard in her recent book, Pop Art, says that this artist's work has nothing to do with Pop Art. Matching the work of Marisol with Asian notions might shed light on this critical divergence while, at the same time, reconsidering the very essence of what is called Pop Art.

Marisol uses what have been called common objects and notable personages in her work. Her materials, techniques and subjects coexist in dynamic relationship. Her work is not narrative and there is no social or political commentary intended. It does not approach the tradition of portraiture or still life. Marisol's art best conforms to the Zen concept of "suchness" or the Tao reference to "being."

> The secret awaits the insight
> Of eyes unclouded by longing
> Those who are bound by desire
> See only the outward container.
>
> Lao Tzu  (tr. R.B. Blakney)

The mystery and tension in her work are caused by the life force carried by the outward container but generated from that which is within.   In her works, whether of adults, babies or objects, the concern is not for their physical appearance but for a universal essence which can be tapped by each individual viewer/participant. Each work is a unique essence just as each viewer is unique.

The Asian concept, yin-yang, operates in Marisol's art. Juxtapositions within materials, forms and subjects and the tension between void/form, joy/sorrow, personal/universal, generate the life/breath of her art. The meaning comes from the space between; the parts are all in a dynamic relationship. The power of her work comes from the mystery of transformation.

Another important element in Marisol's work is the relationship between the universal and the specific. As Shulman stated, "The universal and the specific in Marisol's sculptures seem to be pitted against one another. Between the universal and the specific exist the elements of mystery that can only be pondered, never answered."

From the Asian world view, however, the universal and specific are complements of each other resulting in a living whole;  their interaction is what gives life to a work of art.  Indeed, the mystery, which can only be pondered indeed cannot be answered within the world of rational thought or the dualities of the western tradition.  If taken as a visual koan, however, the pondering can lead to insight and enlightenment but in a place beyond rational thought or logic.  The works of Marisol do not live in a world limited by Western reason or linear logic where there is the expectation of either reality or fantasy, they live in the place between, in the realm of transformation, imagination and insight.

---

[1]Artist's conversation with Gail Gelburd, 12/31/89

Fig. 57. Escobar Marisol, *Shoe and Hand* 1964
Lithograph
25 x 20"
Hofstra Museum Collection, Gift of Dr. Milton Gardner

# Robert Morris

Robert Morris was born in Kansas City and studied engineering at the University of Kansas City. He studied art at both Kansas City Art Institute and the California School of Fine Arts. After moving to New York in 1961, he studied art history at Hunter College, writing a master's thesis on Brancusi. His early career was comprised of a series of performance pieces with dancers such as Yvonne Rainer and Carolee Schneemann. He was tagged a minimalist, along with artists such as Donald Judd, Dan Flavin, Tony Smith and Carl Andre. He was a great admirer of Barnett Newman, an artist deeply concerned with the spiritual in art.

In 1967, Morris began to develop a group of large-scale sculptures, "felt pieces." He was attracted to the "physicality, the presence" of the material. A sense of gravity is achieved in these felt sculptures. Since then, Morris has worked on "earthwork" projects, "scatter" pieces, "space" experiments, and "spill" works. Impressive in size and monumentality, Morris' works demand space.

While his works in the 1960s and 1970s were non-objective, and three-dimensional, he was closely associated with Carl Andre and Walter De Maria, influenced by both John Cage and Merleau Ponty. In a response to a questionnaire sent to the artist in 1984, Morris revealed his intimate knowledge and understanding of Asian philosophy. Each of his experiments with new forms and processes have been ways of reaching inside to our own presence so that as he stated, "Perhaps we can all become Zen masters."[1]

Morris' works of the 1980s are dark in spirit, marked by decorative strength. He developed a way of incorporating painting and architecture into sculpture. In 1981-82 Morris produced a series of cast hydrocal relief works called *Hypnerotomachia*, distinguished by disordered composition, tortuous form, and overall dismal white. The pictures dwell on horror, death, violence, and destruction. "A sense of doom," he said, "has gathered on the horizon of our perception and grows every day."[2] The image of doom is further expressed in the framed works he made in 1983-84, in which violent blacks, yellows, oranges, violets and blues are strongly dumped onto the canvas in swirling lines. A vision of chaos is engendered by the wavelike patterns of the frame. Rich in tension and energy, Morris' works of the 1980s create an atmosphere which oppresses the viewer with a suffocating force. The form, volume, color and image are all integrated into a dramatic whole.

[1] Robert Morris, "Aligned with Nazca" *Artforum* Vol. 14 Oct. 1975.
[2] Robert Morris, *Works of the Eighties* (Chicago: Museum of Contemporary Art, 1986), p. 24.

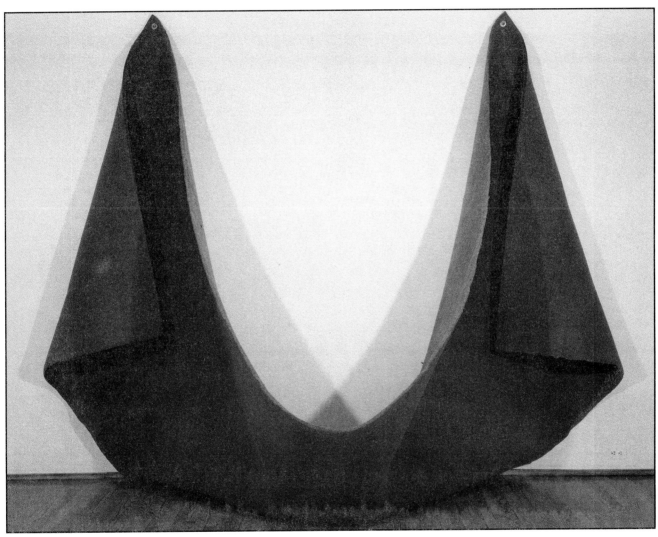

Fig. 58. Robert Morris, *Untitled* 1976
Felt and metal grommets
103 x 132 x 30"
Courtesy The Rivendell Collection

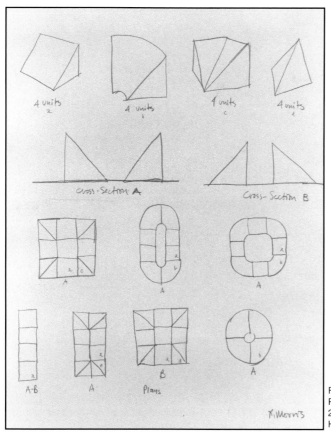

Fig. 59. Robert Morris, *Untitled* 1964
Pencil on paper
20 x 16"
Hofstra Museum Collection; Gift of Diane Kelder

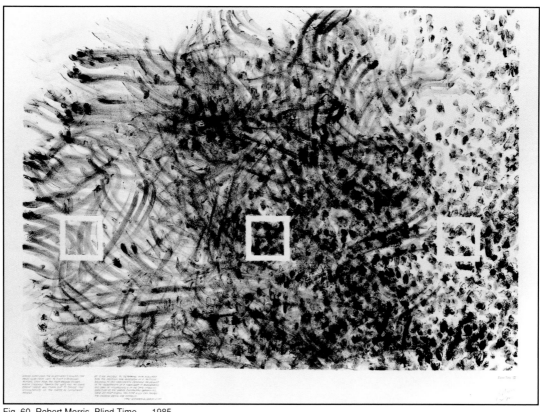

Fig. 60. Robert Morris, Blind Time    1985
Graphite on paper
38 x 50"
Courtesy Leo Castelli Gallery

# Bruce Nauman

Bruce Nauman was born in 1941 in Fort Wayne, Indiana, and grew up in Wisconsin. He studied mathematics and physics at college, until he discovered that art allowed him to use his mind and his hands. His teachers in Wisconsin were artists from the WPA, and they instilled in Nauman a concern for societal issues and the social role of art. From 1964 to 1966, Nauman attended the University of California at Davis, where he studied with Robert Arneson and William Wiley. He soon abandoned painting in favor of three-dimensional art and film art.

In an interview with Jan Butterfield in 1975, Nauman recalls the wealth of influences on him in the late 1960s. He met Philip Glass, read Samuel Beckett and John Cage, and heard the music of Steve Reich and La Monte Young. He was "able to use their idea about time."[1] He read Ludwig Wittgenstein's *Philosophical Investigations* and became increasingly concerned with the process. He embodied Asian philosophical ideas in works such as his film "Fishing for Asian Carp," in which the camera ran as Nauman and his friend William Alan tried to catch a fish. The activity defined the structure of the film and the length of the film. "It was like non-doing," Alan later stated.[2]

Nauman worked in fiberglass and neon, exploring the relationships between his own body and space. In the 1970s he created architectural installations that often incorporated corridor-like spaces video and sound. These works solicited the participation of the viewer. Beginning in the 1980s, Nauman's works dealt with societal issues, though they continued to incorporate psychological components.

From the beginning, Nauman tried to create "art that was there all at once. Like getting hit in the face with a baseball bat."[3] He strives for his art to have the same effect as enlightenment in Zen: it is during the process of the mundane activities of life that the *mystic truths* are revealed.

[1] Jan Butterfield, "Bruce Nauman: The Center of Yourself," *Arts Magazine*, 49 (Feb. 1975), p. 53.
[2] Quoted in Joe Raffaele and Elizabeth Baker, "The Way -Out West: Interviews with Four San Francisco Artists", *Artnews*, Summer 1967, p. 40.
[3] Joan Simon, "Breaking the Silence," *Art In America*, 76 (September 1988), p. 142.

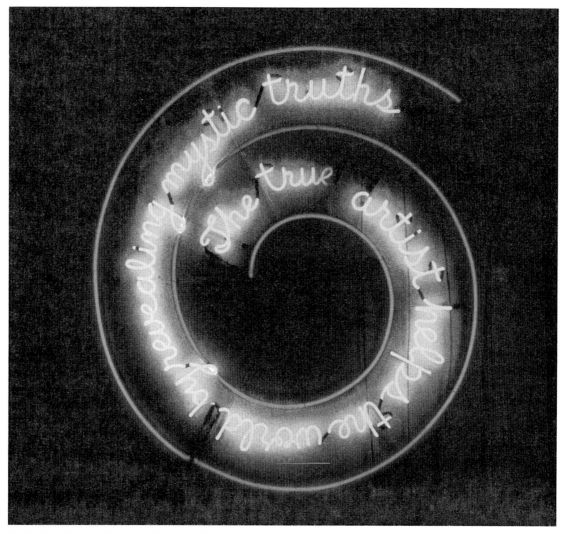

Fig. 61. Bruce Nauman, *Window or Wall Sign* 1967
Blue and peach neon tubing
59 x 55"
Private Collection, (replica) exhibition copy,
Courtesy of Leo Castelli Gallery

# Eric Orr

Eric Orr's introduction to Asian philosophy was through the *Tao Te Ching* in 1956; he pulled the book from a library shelf.[1] His academic training had been in the history of philosophy and economics, not art. "I was 19, hitchhiking from Kentucky to New York City. I got a ride to Philadelphia and got to see the Arensberg collection [of modern art] — by pure chance; I knew nothing about it. I looked at that collection and said, Whew! this is great stuff. In Kentucky art is horses."[2] Later, he considered going to art school, but was appalled by what he saw there and decided to "just do it." He moved to Los Angeles in 1966 and has lived there ever since.

His early works sought to embody many of the ideas in the *Tao Te Ching* with acoustical creations in which the viewer participates in and is surrounded by the art. Orr was trying to convey the idea that art had to be perceived through the mind's eye. In 1970, he decided to take a year off to travel around the world. During this trip, and on subsequent visits, Orr traveled throughout South East Asia and Japan. He has stated that he was most interested in Buddhism before the Buddha. He was fascinated by the stupas; exo-architecture that are to be circumambulated.[3]

When he returned from his trip, he began work on the light pieces for which he has since become best known. Orr has also sought to put the "void" into his paintings. These works are titled *Mu*, which, in Japanese art, are paintings of zero or negative space. In these paintings, a central monochrome area of color washes out to a grey and fades into the background color. The central image seems to float in space. Orr's most recent sculptures are about primal matter, such as fire, water and stone.

---

[1] He was reading an Arthur Waley edition. Interview by Gail Gelburd with Eric Orr, December 20, 1989.
[2] Los Angeles Times, Barbara Martin, "Eric Orr Yokes Power, Rare Sophistication," April 26, 1984.
[3] Interview between Gail Gelburd and Eric Orr, December 1989.

Fig. 62. Eric Orr, *Naked Singularity* 1990
Slate and water
7' 1/2" x 11" x 1 1/2"
Courtesy of the Artist

# Robert Rauschenberg

Born in 1925 Rauschenberg adopted the name "Bob" while studying at the Kansas City Art Institute in the late 1940s. Before art school the U.S. Navy called him to service in 1942, placing him in the Hospital Corps with a position in San Diego, California. From the Kansas City Art Institute to the Academie Julian in Paris to a series of summers at Black Mountain College, North Carolina beginning in 1949, Rauschenberg experienced the rural, the urban and the historical in art and life. In 1949, he and his wife Sasan Weil Rauschenberg chose to settle in New York City where he began attending Art Students League in 1952.

In the summer of 1950 at Black Mountain College, Rauschenberg and John Cage, along with other artists, conceived of the "Happening." At the same time in San Francisco, Seymour Locks, Jess, Jay DeFeo and other Beat artists, Beat poets, and musicians were doing spontaneous performances.[1] "Happenings" are a tutorial on the Zen notion of "direct pointing," insistence on direct experience, and the Buddhist notion of impermanence or transience.

Rauschenberg was influenced by Cage's use of the I-Ching, his Zen notions of the powerful presence of the *void*, and his expressions about the poetic potential in the most common objects. Cage in turn was influenced by Rauschenberg's all-black and all-white paintings.[2] In 1951, Rauschenberg described these paintings as, "dealing with the suspense, excitement and body of an organic silence, the restriction and freedom of absence, the plastic fullness of nothing, the point a circle begins and ends....It is completely irrelevant that I am making them. Today is their Creator."[3]

The statements, "the plastic fullness of nothing" and "Today is their Creator" carry Zen Buddhist and Tao overtones. The attitude signals the conception of the void in an Asian rather than an existential sense. The void is the dynamic, energy-filled, generative space. Rauschenberg's attitudes about Asian thought have matured and today sound less romantic; nevertheless, the alteration of basic conceptions about art and life were permanent.

When Rauschenberg deals with the object it is also in the Zen/Tao sense of reverence for all objects and forms. "I feel sorry for people who think things like soap dishes or mirrors or coke bottles are ugly, because they are surrounded by things like that all day long, and it must make them miserable. There is no poor subject."[4]

Working from a altered world view, catalyzed by Asian notions and practices, Rauschenberg denies the condition of "high art" and "low art" as well as the subject/object dichotomy.. The subject/object fuse to create the potential for experience. Rauschenberg explains, "You should not remember my works because when you leave the room, return, and see them again, they are different because you are different."

Through the 1950s and 1960s Rauschenberg dealt with the conditions of meditation and humor. In the process, he has dissolved the "and." Both types of experience have the potential for altering the consciousness of the viewer/participant; the potential for transformation. Alan Browness said of Rauschenberg's works, "Freudian obsessions are absent and in their place is a more gentle humor."

A partial explanation for the Browness statement lies in the fact that Rauschenberg shares Asian-derived attitudes and practices with his close friends and professional colleagues John Cage, Merce Cunningham and Jasper Johns. Over the years, because of a cross-fertilization of Asian ideas between them, their conception of Asian philosophy has matured as it has been assimilated.[5] The circle of artists, poets, musicians and participants who share this world view has widened exponentially from the 1950s to the present.

---

[1] The Happenings seemed to be a spontaneous and simultaneous development at Black Mountain, San Francisco, and New York. See T. Albright, Art in the San Francisco Bay Area.
[2] See detailed discussion of Cage and Rauschenberg relationship in: R Kostelanetz and M.E. Harris, *The Arts of Black Mountain*, Mass, 1986.
[3] Alan Browness, catalog for an exhibition, Rauschenberg, Tate Gallery.
[4] From text extracted from film "Painters Painting" interview by Emile deAntonio.
[5] From Geri DePaoli conversation with John Cage.

Fig. 63. Robert Rauschenberg, *Link* from Pages and Fuses  1974
Handmade multiple silkscreen on wet paper,
laminated into wet tissue
25 x 20"
Courtesy Gemini G.E.L.

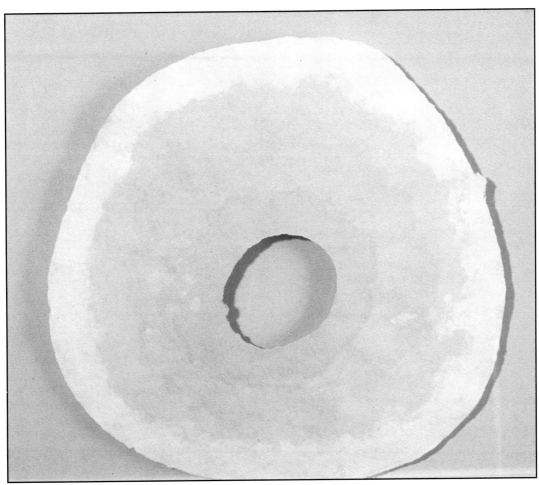

Fig. 64. Robert Rauschenberg, *Pages 2* 1974
Handmade paper print
22 x 22"
Courtesy Gemini G.E.L.

# Larry Rivers

The Beats, Jack Kerouac, John Cage, jazz, abstract expressionism, Funk and Pop Art were all key elements in the artistic environment of Larry Rivers. In 1959, he made the film "Pull My Daisy" with Jack Kerouac, Allen Ginsberg, Robert Frank and others. A Zen/Taoist sense of spontaneity was the key; Rivers performed while Kerouac gave a running commentary. The "poetic essence was so pure that the film was left uncut, un-edited." They had followed the Zen/Tao dictum to "simply be."[1]

Born in 1925 to Samuel and Sonya Grossberg, in 1940, as a jazz saxophonist, he renamed himself Larry Rivers. He first studied music at Juilliard in 1944, and in 1946, after a separation from his wife, he moved to Manhattan and began associating with painters, poets and dancers.

His attitude toward art and life matured in the 1950s in the company of associates such as Ad Reinhardt, along with Phillip Guston and Franz Kline, whom he has acknowledged as influences.[2]

Rivers' was a friend of Kerouac at the time when the author and poet was writing Dharma Bums, and American Buddhist Dharma (never published). Kerouac was reading, studying and discussing Buddhist sutras with Gary Snyder.[3] Allen Ginsberg was exploring and assimilating aspects of Zen and Mahayana Buddhism. Cage, who was deeply involved with Zen study, was frequenting artist gatherings where Buddhist dialogue was common and where Rivers was present.

The nature of consciousness and the relationships between art and life were topics of concern among the 1950s and 1960s literati. The Zen Buddhist and Taoist material that was circulating addressed artists' concerns and acted to give the artists permission to record direct experience and to value that record as art. Asian philosophy validated artists' intuitions and experience.[4]

Rivers was involved in "Happenings" and collaborations on set designs for theater and dance as well as on works of art. Here holistic notions from Asian material not only pertained to individual works of art but applied in the use of music, drama, dance, poetry and visual arts to create a total experience.

Rivers breathed in a Zen air as it was infused by the interpretation and practices of the Beats, the music of John Cage, the dance of Merce Cunningham and the humor and the performances of the 1950s and 1960s. His work emphasized the importance of a focused awareness or direct experience which could lead to transformation.

Rivers said,

> When I was very young and went to the zoo a lot, I once went with my father, who is quite strong. He was feeding a deer through the wire fence and then began playing with the deer's antlers. Suddenly the deer backed away and part of its antlers broke off and there was my father holding them in his hand, and the deer charging off into the distance. Aside from expectations of glory, all I can hope for from my work is that it arrests your attention with no more or less insistence than the breaking of a deer's antlers. That something in my work obliges you to forget for a few moments the absurdity of your life.(Larry Rivers, ArtNews, 60 March 1961, p 55.)

Rivers' work partakes of that Zen attitude of "direct pointing." His love of and participation in jazz makes him even more receptive to the Tao idea of spontaneity and the I-Ching notion of a trust in randomness. His work functions like the Zen koan where the initiate is presented with a statement to ponder which has no basis in logic, no cause and effect relationship.

The alternative world view from Asia in the 1950s and 1960s precipitated a series of re-evaluations and re-alignments in the art community. The result was a (re) placing or recontextualizing of objects and relationships. Artists became receptive to Asian ideas because of rising questions about relationships in nature and/or culture. Rivers, because of his urban experience and his interest in music, literature and poetry, received the ideas through culture. His work is an expression of American-ness and a visual form of Beat Zen.

---

[1]From an interview with Harvey Himelfarb about his knowledge of the filming of Pull My Daisy.
[2]See data on deep involvement with Asian thought by Reinhardt and Guston in: D. Clarke, in an interview by the author with Jane Tilley Griffin, scholar of Asian art, she said that Ad Reinhardt studied Buddhism for a full year in the same class she attended.
[3]Data from research in the archives of Gary Snyder at the University of California, Davis (letters from Kerouac, Ginsberg, Whalen, Kyger, Watts and others).
[4]From an interview by Bill Moyers with Allen Ginsberg on the Public Broadcasting Network, December 1989.

Fig. 65. Larry Rivers, *Ace of Spades* 1980
Oil on canvas
10 x 8"
Private Collection

Fig. 66. Larry Rivers, *The O O from Boom and a Nigerian* 1968
Mixed media
11 x 14"
Private Collection

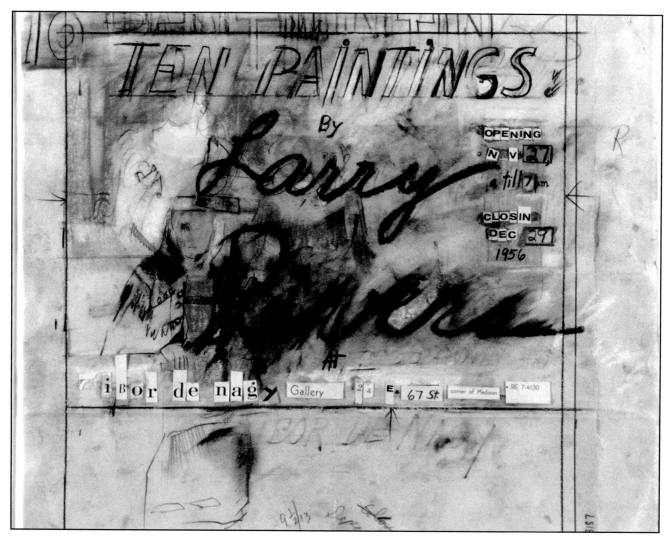

Fig. 67. Larry Rivers, *Poster for Exhibition at Tibor de Nagy* 1956
Pastel
14 x 16 1/2"
Private Collection

Fig. 68. Larry Rivers, *F for Flower* 1971
Mixed media
14 x 16"
Private Collection

# James Rosenquist

After he had studied art in Minnesota and at the Art Students League in New York, in 1957, James Rosenquist shared a studio in the city, met Rauschenberg and Johns and became interested in the works of Jackson Pollock and Sam Francis. He worked as an industrial painter and a chauffeur to support himself and had his first one-man show in 1962. He shared the interest in Zen, Tao and a wide variety of Asian material and practices with the whole art community in New York during the 1950s and 1960s. Rosenquist also studied Asian thought at the Aspen Institute for Humanistic studies in 1965 and visited Japan in 1966. In his statements about his work one can identify code words for the Asian material.

> The imagery of the sixties may have had to do with the Beat generation and the rejection of material things. Remember the abundance of material things in the 1950s? The look of the front end of new automobiles was a vacant vision, like "direct emptiness." Painting the front end of an automobile wasn't concerned with nostalgia. I had an abstract attitude toward my painting.[1]

The phrase "direct emptiness" is a Zen term; it is what Zen aims for, the active void which is described in many texts on Buddhism and specifically Zen. It describes the space in a work of art in a way which is a radical departure from past Western references to "negative space." Interpretations of Rosenquist's works have tended to be complex and confusing because critics have tried to match his work with the characteristics of a traditional Western system wherein when a object is represented, the meaning is directly connected to the object; it functions as a substitute for the "real thing."

In his works Rosenquist presents powerful active voids. The relationships of the forms and voids take place in physical and psychological space. The subject is not the object; the works function as Zen "direct pointing," pointing the viewer back to himself. Each work functions as a "Happening" for each viewer. No narrative, social or political statement is intended nor is there an expectation of a logical conclusion. The subject of the object is experience. His works say forcefully, "Don't mistake the finger for the moon," and the works follow the Buddhist notion of no grasping, no expectations but rather exist as "suchness."

Rosenquist reaffirms, "I wanted the space to be more important than the imagery. I wanted to use images as tools. But it just didn't happen because the dumb critics said, 'Oh look, I can recognize that, that's a car, that's a hot dog, that's popular.' My work didn't have anything to do with popular images like chewing gum!"[2]

The experience of Rosenquist's works can best be described, as is the case with many works from Pop Art, as visual koans. He presents images and parts of images in random and paradoxical association and their juxtaposition leads beyond reason, beyond thought. The viewer is left to ponder and cannot draw meaning or insight from any outside prescriptions or set of laws but only from within the self. Considering the statements from the artist and looking at his works one sees that space, time and humor in the works are compatible with the Asian notions of those elements.

[1] J. Rosenquist: Interview by Phyllis Tuchman, ArtNews, May 1974 (p. 28).
[2] Judith Goldman, *James Rosenquist*, NY 1985, p35.

Fig. 69. James Rosenquist, *Wind and Lightening* 1975
Charcoal, silver paint and gouache
36 x 71 1/4"
Courtesy Carole and Alex Rosenberg

# Carolee Schneemann

Carolee Schneemann has been thoroughly acquainted with Zen, Tao and I-Ching material since her life in art began in the 1960s.[1] She says that once a person takes in these ideas, it changes his/her whole life. The consequences of her experience with Asian philosophy can be seen in her work with its Zen type of humor and with a Tao naturalness and spontaneous quality.

Her work speaks of nature and culture. Whether it addresses the issue of war or aesthetics, there is a trust and matter-of-factness that recognizes processes and conditions as natural events. Her works point to life's conditions without preaching or judgment. She provides the viewer with an experience which often leads to heightened awareness and new perspectives.

A Zen/Tao attitude can be seen in works as diverse as "War Mop," where a mop is propelled by a plexiglass wheel to continually beat on a television set; or *Cluny Ladder* (Fig. 70) where a panel covered with mixed media and lit by two poles at each side allows the viewer to see forms which seem to appear and disappear; and the *Dust Paintings* (Fig.13), where the work is created by the acceptance of random or chance occurrence.

In her paintings, constructions, and happenings she follows the Zen dictum, "no one thing more important than another." From it comes an affirmation of the choice of objects and fragments previously neglected or assigned outcast status. There is no hierarchy of materials or subject matter. All parts function in harmony with the whole work. Order is found, not imposed, and there is no expectation of conclusion.

She addresses war themes as a condition of disharmony which she points out with paradox and humor in the Zen spirit of "suchness." In "Viet Flakes," a video performance, she describes war, " a condition as 'randomized', as constant, as weather."[2]

Her work has been called "classic," perhaps because it possesses a timelessness and spirit-energy, that mysterious quality of all life. Her exposure to the Tao and its explication of the mysterious female nature also affirms her celebration of the sensual and sexuality in the Tao spirit of naturalness, spontaniety and humor, rising above the sexual or sexist Western taboos.

The following is a statement from Carolee Schneemann (letter to the author December 1989) Lao Tzu was absorbed, claimed as a poet/wise man sometime between 1000 and 600 B.C., when priestesses, philosophers, physicians, artists, poets were appropriated as male entities. The legend that he was born white-haired after sixty-two years in his mother's womb resembles other appropriation/origin legends in which a female source loses gender preeminence as part of the historic masculine struggle for cultural dominance.

In the 1960s, I threw sticks to ask the I-Ching why its gender referents were all masculine (I-Ching who are you?) I received Kuei Mei/ The Marrying Maiden..six at the top... (the woman holds the basket, but there are no fruits in it) and (I am not what I appear to be..) Some past research fragments inform gender inversions in the I-Ching; for instance, the sun had been a female attribute in earlier versions. With the Wilhelm translation, all third person pronouns are masculine; so one has to wonder if the shifting of gender attributes occurred with the tyrant Ch'in Shih Huang Ti, after the followers of Confucius had been influenced by the Book of Changes, or with the Baynes translation from Wilhelm?"

Carolee Schneemann has had a long and distinguished career and has produced works which defy all boundries of classification. Painting, construction, collage, sculpture, film, performance, writing are all expressions of the same "Way" or spirit. Her art, each individual work and the whole body of her work, subscribes to the spirit of the Tao:

> Words came out of the womb of matter;
> And whether a man dispassionately
> Sees to the core of life
> Or passionately
> Sees the surface,
> The core and the surface
> Are essentially the same,
> Words making them different
> Only to express appearance.
> If name be needed, wonder names them
>  both:
> From wonder to wonder
> Existence opens.

*The Way of Life* according to Lao Tzu
tr. by Witter Bynner, 1944.

[1] Personal interview with the G. DePaoli.
[2] Julia Ballerini, *Carolee Schneemann: Recent Work*, Documenta text 1983.

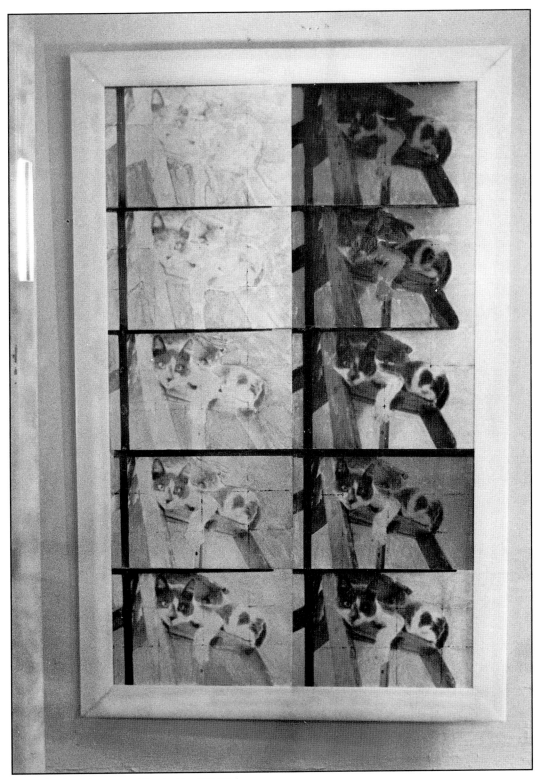

Fig. 70. Carolee Schneemann, *Cluny Ladder* 1981-83
Itec photo prints, acrylic paint, glass, particle board
115 3/4 and 36"
Collection of the Artist

# Richard Serra

Encouraged by his parents, Richard Serra began to draw and paint in his early adolescence. He studied English literature at the University of California, Santa Barbara and art at the Yale School of Art and Architecture. At Yale, he studied with Robert Rauschenberg, Frank Stella and Philip Guston. It was Rauschenberg and Guston who directed Serra to the philosophies of the Orient. His understanding of Asian thought was enhanced when he formed a close relationship with Philip Glass while visiting Paris in 1964. The music of Philip Glass has been influential to Serra. While travelling in Paris on a fellowship from Yale, he cemented his friendship with Glass and then became acquainted with Steve Reich, Michael Snow (composer and filmmaker), Sol LeWitt and Walter de Maria, Eva Hesse, Carl Andre and Robert Smithson (who all congregated downstairs at Max's Kansas City).

Influenced by John Cage's ideas about the role of chance in art, Serra produced a number of works in which paint was adopted as a "found object." Serra began to incorporate objects like stones, sticks, or branches into his work.

Serra was drawn to Brancusi. While in Paris, he would go to Brancusi's reconstructed atelier to sketch. His interest in Brancusi, however, is not of Brancusi's *Endless Column* (1918) which so many other American artists were attracted to. Serra stated of Constantin Brancusi's *Endless Column:*

> The fact that it measured a definite space from floor to ceiling anticipates Judd's thinking from floor to ceiling, and what Andre had done from wall to wall. The idea of the infinite implied by the module extension was most impressive in Brancusi. It changed the sensibility of the entire sixties...Stella's black pictures and Judd's serial relationships are indebted to the *Endless Column*. But the problems in the *Endless Column* didn't interest me at that time. I was more interested in Brancusi's open pieces, like the *Gate of the Kiss.*[1]

Serra is concerned with the pressure of oppositions found in *The Kiss.* Brancusi is continually dealing with the Gestalt, the whole and the way it is broken up. The solid block of *The Kiss* is split by the opposing forces, the *yin* and *yang,* the male and the female.

Merleau-Ponty (translated in 1962) also pointed the way for this generation to see not figuration, but the spatiality of things and Asian philosophy. Serra engaged in several sculptural experiments during his career: rubber, neon, and metal works, 1966-67; molten and cast lead works, 1968-69; he created temporal cut and torn pieces, 1968-71; propped or weighted leaning pieces, 1968-71 and experimental films, 1968-77 that dealt with issues of perception and reality. (Serra was an astute student of the precision of Russian films by Eisenstein, Dziga Vertov, Pudhovkin and Alexander Dovzhenko.)

Serra has created numerous large scale site-specific works such as *St. John's Rotary Arc.* Made of large steel plates, they dominate the site, yet direct the movement of the visitor/participant. The *Prop* pieces maintain a tenuous balance that makes it seem as if it is always changing, yet calm. Serra's work is always about the context in which it is placed and has a physical presence. He has stated that the pieces he creates are not monuments or monumental except in concept.

[1] Rosalind Krauss, "Richard Serra," *Richard Serra*, NY: Museum of Modern Art, 1986.

Fig. 71. Richard Serra, *Cape Breton Prop* 1988
Corten steel
60 x 60 x 2" plate, 54 x 7" diameter bar
The Rivendell Collection

# Michael Singer

Michael Singer's sculptures first received major exposure at the Guggenheim exhibition *Ten Young Artists: Theodoron Awards* in 1971. These early works evolved out of Minimalism, particularly Carl Andre's floor pieces and Serra's lead-prop pieces, in which the object confronts the viewer in an aggressive way. Andre's works were considered "as level as water" and identified the floor as their plane. Serra's works were about balance, gravity and the materials. Singer admits that these ideas coalesced in his works. Singer shared with these artists a concern for process, an interest in the materials, and Asian philosophy.

Michael Singer's understanding of Eastern philosophical ideas is displayed even in his earliest works. The first of his sculptures, dating from 1969-70 were made of steel and milled wood. In 1971, he began working outdoors with wind-felled logs to create a group of pieces called *Situation Balances*, devoted to a veneration of nature and a commitment to transience. Singer, like many other artists in this exhibition, preserved the fundamental doctrine of Zen: a respect for Nature.

After *Situation Balances*, Singer continued to create art out-of-doors, composed of grasses and twigs and oriented to the specific site. (He did not return to an indoor gallery setting until 1977.) His work sought to show the harmonious yet precarious balance of nature. Singer was greatly influenced by Alan Kaprow at Cornell University, where Singer was studying in 1964. A year later, he transferred to New York University at Stony Brook, where Kaprow usually taught. He performed in Kaprow's happening called "Household." Kaprow's experimental approach inspired Singer, who began to create works of art related to the environment. He looked to the salt marshes of Long Island and other unspoiled areas. He has written of the "remarkable harmony between the people of Lake Titicaca, Peru and their environment," and has looked at Zen architecture. His own architectural work concerns the relationship between indoor and outdoor spaces and shows his sensitive use of natural materials and his ability to transcend the utilitarian.

Concerned not only with a reverence for nature but with ritual as well, like magical ceremonies, his environments function as adjusters, keeping balance within the total milieu... In the largest sense they are ecological, dealing with interpenetrating systems — with man's continuity, with nature's flow and his position in its web.

Fig. 72. Michael Singer, *Ritual Series 11/9/78* 1978
Paper, collage, charcoal and chalk on paper
43 5/8 x 31 5/8"
Collection of the Artist

# Michelle Stuart

Michelle Stuart's work is based on her approach to the themes of nature, man, earth, and time. Nature for her is an "inextricable part of her universe which must be accepted, not challenged"[1] a Zen world view.

Born in Los Angeles, Stuart came from an immigrant Australian family. Her father was a cartographical engineer. She recalls in her childhood that she accompanied him to the seashores and vast deserts of California and to inland regions, where she later found vital sources for her art. After art school, Stuart worked as a topographical draftswoman, but also began making both figurative and abstract works. In 1968, Stuart began to produce a series of drawings based on studies of the moon's surface. There followed several series of drawings which documented changes in nature.

Stuart has been preoccupied with the "divine powers" of stones and rocks. She has used two major forms in her most recent work: "rock books" and "stone scrolls." "They are `histories' of a place," Stuart remarked about her rock books. The soil and gravel used for these books are records of her voyages to distant places. She has visited Japan, Morocco, and Lapland, making a particular point of travelling to ancient sites to study monuments and rituals. Stuart has read the kamasutra and books about Asian philosophy. After visiting Nepal and participating in a series of ceremonies, she found that the Buddhist way of thought was transcending and more accepting of differences among people. Inspired by Japanese scrolls, Stuart made stone scrolls in a monumental formation composed of large paper sheets. They flow from the wall to the floor like "ladders to the universe." In that flow, she catches the essence of continuity, the eternal rhythm within the universe. In contrast, her intimate and fragile books have subtle graduations of muted color and textures. The simple images, bound together, are histories without words. *Book of Stones* (Fig.73) combines *book* and *nature*. Stuart collects rocks (as does John Cage and Patricia Johanson) and finds in each one unique histories layered with time. Her most recent paintings imbed time and place into the art.

---

[1] Robert Hobbs, *Michelle Stuart*, exhibition catalogue (Cambridge: Hayden Gallery, 1977).

Fig. 73. Michelle Stuart, *Book of the Stone* 1984/85
Earth, hydrocal, linen, encaustic, and muslin
9 x 9 x 2 1/2"
Courtesy Fawbush Gallery

# William T. Wiley

Through de-mystifying established hierarchies, re-mystifying the most common of objects, William Wiley's work follows the Zen dictum, "one thing no more important than another." This attitude is also in concert with the overall Buddhist notion of reverence for all things....the respect and acknowledgment that everything has a life quality or life nature, its "ness," at the same time realizing the impermanence of all things and the condition of flux. Also in keeping with the Asian world view, Wiley believes that within every experience lies an ocean of possibilities. Anything can serve as an opening or door to enlightenment or satori.

The viewer/participant's response to Wiley's work can be likened to a satori experience in that it elicits a sudden perception or deep insight into the life-nature of all things. In the most ordinary, and at the same time, the most unexpected combination, there is the poetry, the door to transformation.

Wiley's journey in art began at an early age and it was mapped out in high school with the direction and encouragement of his teacher Jim McGrath. It was also at this time that he became acquainted with Zen/Tao attitudes. As he says, "I guess my first experience (with Zen and Tao) came because of an attitude about nature. Don't forget I grew up in the state of Washington, near the site of the first atomic plant. If you live through that kind of experience, you begin to think about a relationship to nature in different ways."[1]

At this time the art of Arp, Klee, Morris Graves and Mark Tobey were important to him. His exposure to Asian art came through class visits to Seattle museums and on less frequent trips to San Francisco and Los Angeles. The ideas and the art of Asia entered his consciousness quite early. (In this sense, his experience parallels that of Jackson Pollock who was taken by his high school teacher to hear Krishnamurti speak and maintained an interest in Asian thought from that time.)

In 1956, when Wiley began studies at the San Francisco Art Institute he heard lectures on Zen/Tao by Alan Watts and he cites two texts, *Zen Flesh, Zen Bones*, by Paul Reps and *Zen Mind, Beginners Mind* by Shunryu Suzuki as important sources for him.

Wiley's aesthetic sensibility grew in the company of fellow students and teachers including; Frank Lobdell, Manuel Neri, Bill Allan, and Joan Brown. He says that he, like many in the Bay Area, was touched by the aftereffects of Still. In the art of assemblage and in ideas about the Tao his awareness of Seymour Locks, artist and highly influential teacher of many Bay area artists, was most significant. Duchamp became a strong influence for Wiley and when asked how the French master and Zen ideas compared, he said, " For me Duchamp was Zen." New York critic Dore Ashton's 1958 analysis of Wiley's work might be aptly subtitled, "art as koan."

> ...the expressionist blur which softens forms and makes their surfaces vibrate; and a stress on asymmetry and diagonal dynamism. He also joined some of the younger artists in the incorporation of emblematic Americana, stars and stripes, and ambiguous symbols of popular culture...Wiley's own personality is expressed in his use of almost-readable symbols.

"Almost readable symbols" sets Wiley's work and his use of Zen and the I-Ching in the same context as that of John Cage who takes fragments of words, phrases, sounds and recombines them according to chance, using humor as a prism to allow for new perspectives and perceptions. As long as one remains tied to predetermined expectations and appearances, there is no meaning in these works. Once one is open to recognizing, instead of imposing, a single fixed meaning, the potential is unending.

Wiley insists on direct experience. He subscribes to the attitude of the Zen master who says that to talk of putting a finger in boiling water is much different from actually doing it. His work functions like Zen koan practice, there are riddles and puzzles, it is based on his perception of his own experience. In the spirit of what often seems to the Western mind an enigmatic Zen attitude, Wiley says, "I am my own enigma."

In the 1960s and 1970s he taught at the University of California at Davis, where he exchanged ideas about Asian thought in lively sessions with his colleagues. Now as he continues to create and experience, when asked about his source of Asian ideas, "I continue to get a lot from my wife; she is a primary source of these ideas for me."

---

[1] From telephone conversation between the artist and Geri DePaoli.

Fig. 74,75. William Wiley, *Beatnik Meteor* 1970
Wooden box containing multiple objects and drawings
60 x 28 x 7"
Rene and Veronica di Rosa Foundation

Fig. 76. William Wiley, *In Time for Spring Cleaning* 1967
Construction
60 x 28 x 7"
Collection, Renee and Veronica di Rosa

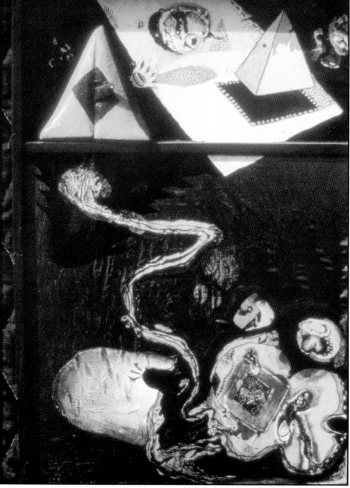

Fig. 77. William Wiley,
*Hidden Power* 1962
Mixed media construction: paint on
wood and paper
17 1/4 x 11 1/4 x 1 3/4"
Collection, Rene and Veronica di Rosa

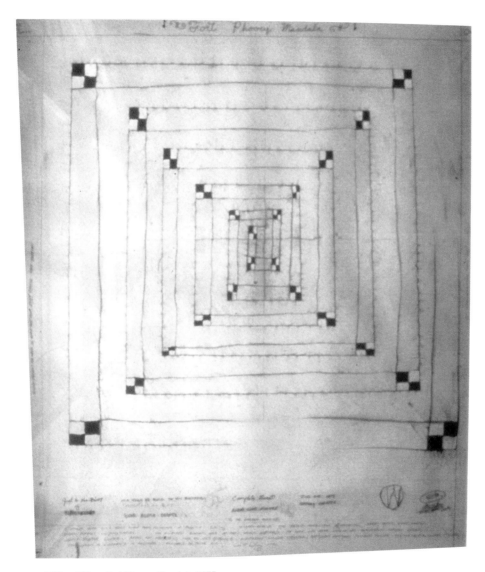

Fig. 78. William Wiley, *Fort Phooey Mandala* 1975
Mixed media on paper
36 x 23"
Collection, Rene and Veronica di Rosa

# Christopher Wilmarth

The art of Christopher Wilmarth began to develop in the atmosphere of Minimalism, but he found that his own inclinations were toward an art that was more intuitive and expressive, less formal. He discovered that the spirituality in Eastern philosophy, as conveyed by Tony Smith and Brancusi and Mallarmé, was suited to his philosophical needs.

Wilmarth was born in Sonoma, California, in 1943. In 1960, he moved to New York City and began to study art at Cooper Union. He was drawn to Brancusi's rough hewn wood and polished sculptures and to the figure studies of Henri Matisse.

For two years, Wilmarth worked as an assistant for Tony Smith, helping him to build, install and paint prototypes. He also greatly admired Joseph Paxton, the architect of the Crystal Palace, and Maurice Marinot, a French creator of blown glass. Wilmarth's early works were layered and painted wall pieces of canvas, paper, wood and wire.

In 1967, Wilmarth began to work in glass. His earliest glass pieces were composed of unpainted spools and partial cylinders of birch plywood sliced by plate glass. After working on a collaborative piece with Mark di Suvero, Wilmarth began to use steel with the glass. His best known works are a set of blown-glass pieces created in response to the poetry of Mallarmé. Wilmarth found a special affinity with the poet and philosopher, Mallarmé. He found in Mallarmé a cross between Asian concepts and Western literature.[1] From 1979 to 1983, Wilmarth created blown glass sculptures, drawings and watercolors as illustrations for Mallarmé poems. The drawing and water colors are equally revealing in their simplicity. His last works, before his death in 1987, are dark and dramatic and might be compared in spirituality to Mark Rothko's late grey paintings.

Wilmarth's sculpture, be they steel plates or blown glass dissolve the objectness of the form. Through the austere yet subtle use of shadows his works become the paradigm of form/void, void/form relationships. Similarly, his works on paper capture with simple lines, the active void. They direct us inward. Light, inward and outward, is captured in glass and on paper and steel. In a catalogue titled *Nine Clearings For a Standing Man* he wrote:

> Light gains character as it touches the world; from what is lighted and who is there to see. I associate the significant moments of my life with the character of the light at the time. The universal implications of my original experience are located in and become signified by kinds of light. My sculptures are places to generate this experience compressed into light and shadow and return them to the world as a physical poem.

[1] Discussion between Gail Gelburd and the artist, 1985.

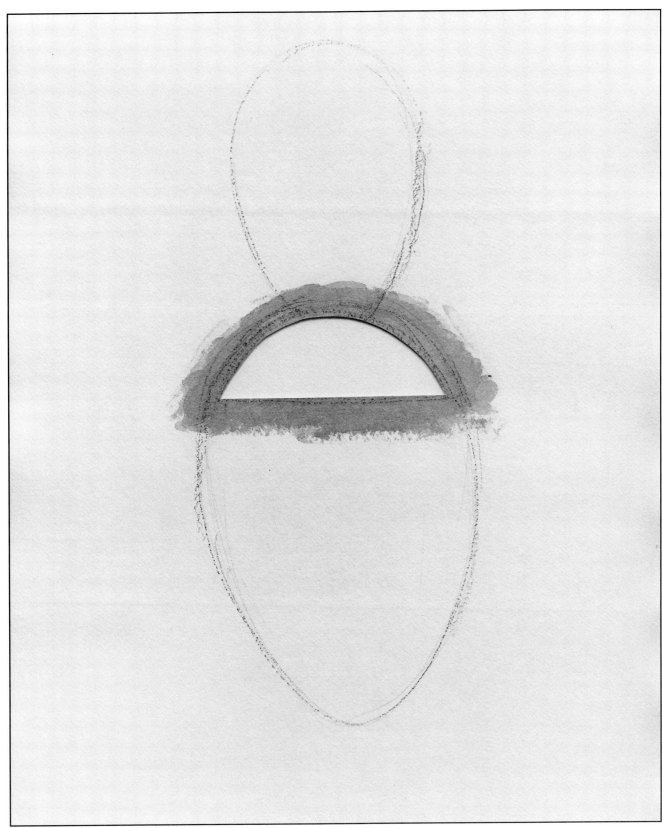

Fig. 79. Christopher Wilmarth, *My Old Books Closed* c 1979
Watercolor, charcoal and graphite on paper
31 x 22 3/8"
Courtesy Hirschl & Adler Modern

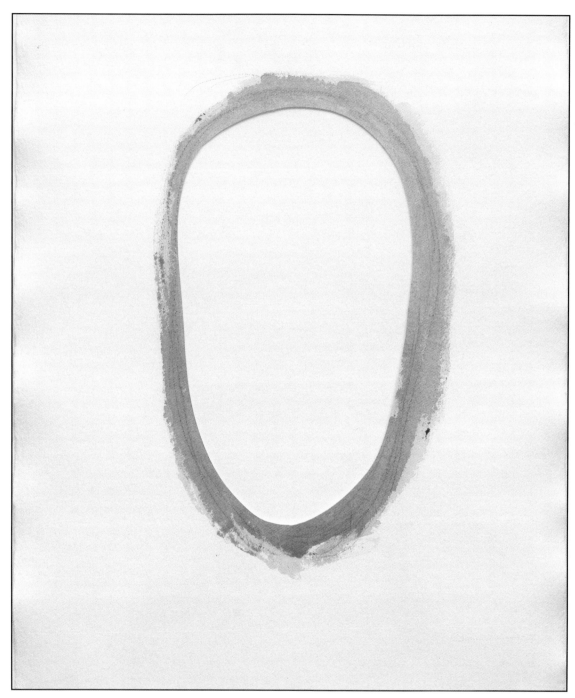

Fig. 80. Christopher Wilmarth, *Sigh* c 1979
Watercolor, charcoal, graphite on paper
31 x 22 3/8"
Courtesy Hirschl & Adler Modern

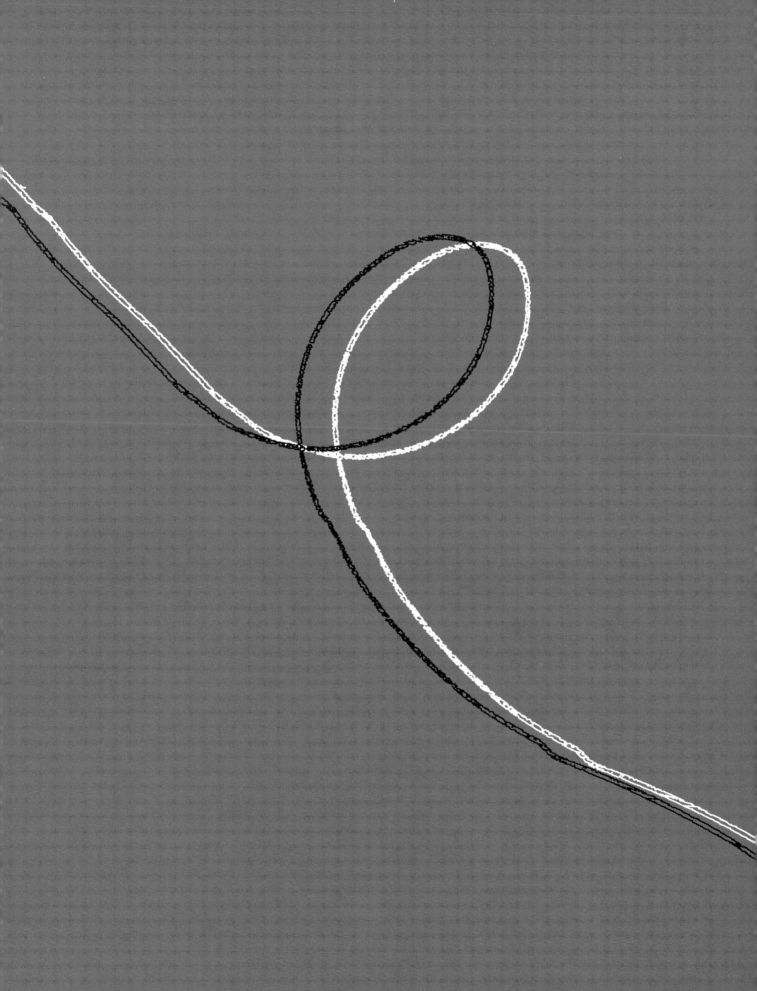

119

# Bibliography

Abe, Masao. ed by Wm. R. LaFleur *Zen and Western Thought*, University of Hawaii Press, 1985.

Adams, Hugh. *Art of the Sixties*. Oxford, 1978.

Adams, Hugh. "Sixty Seasons". *Third Eye Center*. Glasgow, Jan. 1983.

Albright, Thomas. *Art in the San Francisco Bay/Area*, 1945-1980, University of California Press, 1985.

Alloway, Lawrence. *Rauschenberg*, Washington, DC, 1977.

Ames, VanMeter. *Zen and American Thought*, Honolulu, 1962.

Ando, Shoei. *Zen and American Transcendentalism*. Tokyo: Hokuseido Press, 1970.

Apostolos-Cappadonna, Diane. ed. *Art Creativity and the Sacred,* Crossroad New York, 1984.

Armstrong, Tom; Craven Wayne; Feder, Norman; et al. *200 Years of American Sculpture*. Whitney Museum of American Art New York: 1976.

Ashton, Dore. *The New York School: A Cultural Reckoning*, NY 1971.

Auping, Michael. *Jess: Paste Ups and Assemblies 1951-1983*, Ringling Museum of Art, 1984.

*Baldessari, John.* essays by Marcia Tucker, Robert Pincus-Whitten, New Museum 1981 (catalog).

Beckett, L.C. *Neti Neti: Not This Not That*, Watkins, London 1959.

Blakney, R.B. *The Way of Life: Lao Tzu,* Mentor, New York 1955.

Beal, Graham and Perreault John. *Wiley Territory,* Minneapolis, Walker Art Center, 1979.

Blinder, David. "The Controversy Over Conventionalism", *The Journal of Aesthetics and Art Criticism* XL Spring, 1983.

Bohm, David. *Wholeness and the Implicate Order,* ARK London, 1980.

Bognar, Botond. "The Japanese Order of Things" *Pratt Journal of Architecture*, Vol. 2, Spring 1988, pp.148-162.

Booker, Christopher. The 70's: *The Decade That Changed the Future*. NY: Stein and Day, 1980.

Bourdon, David. "Walter De Maria: The Singular Experience". *Art International.* Vol.12, December 1968, pp.39-43.

Bryson, Norman. *Vision and Painting,* New Haven, 1983.

Butterfield, Jan. "Bruce Nauman: The Center of Yourself", *Arts Magazine,* 49 (Feb 1975) p.53.

Cage, John. *Silence,* Middletown, 1961.

Cage, John. *A Year From Monday,* Middletown, 1967.

Calas, Nicolas. *Icons and Images of the 60's.* N.Y.: EP Dutton, 1971.

Campbell, Joseph. *Man and Transformation: Papers from the Eranos Yearbooks,* Princeton University Press, 1964.

Campbell, Joseph. *The Hero With a Thousand Faces.* New York, 1953.

Capra, Fritjof. *The Tao of Physics.* Toronto: Bantan Books, 1984.

*Chicago Review , "Zen"* (Suzuki, Watts, Kerouac, Samuel Beckett) University of Chicago, 1958.

Chisolm, L.W. *Fenollosa: The Far East and American Culture,* New Haven, 1963.

Clarke, David J. *The Influence of Oriental Thought on Postwar American Painting and Sculpture,* Garland, NY, 1988.

Conze, Edward. *Buddhism: Its Essence and Development.* N.Y.: Harper and Row, 1975.

Coomaraswamy, Ananda K. *The Transformation of Nature in Art,* New York, 1956.

Coplans, John. *"Angel-Hipsterism Beat and Zen Versus New Materials",* Artforum Vol.1 No.4, September 1962, pp.39-42. POP Art USA Oaklnad Art Museum, 1963.

De Paoli, Geri, "Jane Teller's Sculpture and Drawings! Powerful Presences in the Big Rhythm", *Woman's Art Journal,* Spring 1987.

Deshimaru, Taisen. *Questions to a Zen Master,* Dutton, 1985.

*Dictionary of Literary Biography,* ed. Ann Charters, Vol. 16 I and II Beat Literature, Mich. 1983.

Dillenberger, Jane. *Perceptions of the Spirit: Spirituality in Art 1900-1970.* University of California Berkely.

Eliade, Mircea. *The Sacred and the Profane: The Nature of Religion* Trans. Summer 1961.

Ellwood, Robert S. Jr. *Alternate Altars: Unconventional and Eastern Spirituality in America,* University of Chicago Press 1979.

Engel, David H. *Japanese Gardens For Today.* (Vermont: Tuttle Co., 1959), p. 13.

Fields, Rick. *How the Swans Came to the Lake.* Co: Shambhala, 1981.

Fong, Wen C. *Modern Art and Chinese Criticism,* Paper given at the National Museum, Taipei, 1988.

Fried, Michael. "Art and Objecthood". *Artforum.* 1967.

Friedman, Lenore. *Meetings With Remarkable Women: Women in Buddhist Practice in America.* San Francisco, 1989.

Geertz, Clifford. *The Interpretation of Culture,* Basic Books NY 1973.

Gelburd, Gail. *Far Eastern Philosophical Influences on Environmental Art,* CUNY. UMI Press, 1988.

Gelburd, Gail. *Androgyny In Art.* NY: Hofstra University, 1982.

Giles, Herbert A. *Chuang Tzu,* London, Quaritch 1926.

Goossen, E.C. *Art of the Real.* N.Y.: MOMA, 1968.

Goossen, E.C. "The Big Canvas". *Art International.* 1958.

Goossen, E.C. "The End of the Object". *Art International.* 1959.

Gottlieb, Carla. *Beyond Modern Art.* NY: Dutton, 1976.

Gudmunsen, Chris. *Wittgenstein and Buddhism* 1977, reprinted in 1986 London (Macmillan ed. ltd.)

Hansen, Al. *A Primer of Happenings and Time/Space Art* NY 1965.

Harrison, Helen A. *Larry Rivers,* Harper and Row NY 1977.

Hawkins, B. "Contemporary Art and the Orient", *College Art Journal,* Vol. XVI.

Heath, Jim F. *The Decade of Disillusionment: The Kennedy-Johnson Years.* Indiana U. Press.

Henderson, L.D. *The Fourth Dimension and Non-Euclidian Geometry in Modern Art,* Princeton University Press, 1983.

Herrigel, Eugen. *Zen in the Art of Archery.* New York, 1953.

Highet, Gilbert. *The Classical Tradition: Greek and Roman Influences on Western Literature,* Oxford University Press 1949.

Hockney, David. *On Photography,* Andre Emmerich Gallery NY 1983.

Hoover, Thomas. *Zen Culture, Japanese Culture.* NY: Random House, 1977.

Howe, Irving and Michael Harrington. *The Seventies: Problems and Proposals.* New York: Harper and Row, 1972.

Hughes, Robert. "Poetry of Emptiness". *Time.* Vol.117, (Jan 5, 1981, p.81).

Humphreys, Christmas. *Zen Comes West: The Present and Future of Zen Buddhism in Western Society,* Curzon Press, London 1977.

Irwin, Robert. *Being and Circumstance, Notes Toward a Conditional Art.* Cal: Lapis Press, 1985.

Jackson, Carl, T. *Oriental Religions and American Thought: 19th Century Explorations,* Greenwood, 1981.

Jung, Carl, G. *Psychology and Religion: West and East,* London 1958.

Kegenick, Coen. "Minimal and Conceptual Ausder Sammlung Panze?". *Kuntswerk.* Vol.34, No.1, 1981, p.59.

Kepes, Gyorgy. *Arts of the Environment.* NY: George Braziller, 1972.

Kerouac, Jack. *Meditation in the Woods,* Chicago Review Vol. 12 no.2, 1958.

Kodama, Sanehide. *American Poetry and Japanese Culture,* Anchor Books, 1984.

Kostelanetz, Richard. *John Cage.* NY: Praeger, 1970.

Kuhn, Thomas. *The Essential Tension: Selected Studies in Scientific Tradition and Change,* University of Chicago, 1977.

Kutner, Janet. "Los Angeles in the 70's", *Art News* 76 (Dec. 1977), p. 104.

Lancaster, Clay. *The Japanese Influence on America.* NY: Walton Rawls Pub., 1963. 2nd ed. NY: Abbeville Press, 1983.

Lao, Tzu. *Tao Te Ching.* Baltimore: Penguin Books, Ltd., 1963.

Leach, Bernard. *Beyond East and West.* London, 1978.

Lee, Sherman. *Past, Present, East and West.* NY: Braziller, 1983.

Lippard, Lucy. "Microcosm to Macrocosm." *Artforum.* Vol.12, Feb. 1974, pp.36-39.

Lippard, Lucy, R. *Pop Art,* New York, 1988.

Lippard, Lucy R. *Six Years: The Dematerialization of the Art Object From 1966 to 1972.* New York: Praeger Publishers, 1973.

Lipsey, Roger. *An Art of Our Own,* Shambhala, 1988.

Mahsun, Carol Anne. *Pop and the Critics,* UMI Press 1987.

Masheck, Joseph. "A Note on Surrealism and the Beats" *Artforum,* XVI8 (Apr 1977) 58-59. adapted from catalog essay, *Beat Art* Butler Library, Columbia University.

McEvilley, Thomas. "Negative Presences in Secret Spaces: The Art of Eric Orr" *Artforum* 20 (Summer 1982), p.58-66.

McGrath, Thomas. "Bear Shit on the Trail Group", *Centrum (Journal)* Fort Worden State Park, Port Townsend WA 98368.

Merleau-Ponty, Maurice. *The Phenomenology of Perception.* Paris: 1945; Trans. by Colin Smith, London, 1962.

Merton, Thomas. *Zen and the Birds of Appetite*, New York 1968.

Monte, James and Marsha Tucker. *Anti-Illusion: Procedures/ Materials.* Whitney Museum, May 19-July 6, 1969.

Morris, Robert. "Aligned with Nazca" *Artforum*, Vol 14, Oct. 1975, p. 39.

Munro, Eleanor. Originals: *American Women Artists.* NY: Simon and Schuster, 1979.

Museum of Modern Art, *Christopher Wilmarth,* N.Y., 1989, p.14.

Northrop. Esc. *The Meeting of East and West.* NY: MacMillan Co., 1946.

O'Connor, Frances and Thaw E. *Jackson Pollock, Catalogue Raisonné of Paintings and Drawings and Other works,* New Haven and London, 1978.

Oden, Steve. Hua Yen *Buddhism and Process Metaphysics.*

Onslow-Ford, *Creation,* Basel 1978.

Ornstein, R. E. *The Mind Field,* 1976. NY: Grossman Pub., 1976.

Paoletti, John T. *The Critical Eye*, I. New Haven: Yale Center for British Art, 1984.

Pearlstein, Phillip. "When Paintings Were Made in Heaven" *Art in America.* Feb. 1982. pp.84-95.

Phillips, Bernard, ed. *The Essentials of Zen Buddhism, Anthology of DT Suzuki.* NY: Dutton, 1962.

Pincus-Witten, Robert. "Serra: Slow Information". *Artforum.* Vol. 8, No.1, Sept. 1969.

Pirsig, Robert. *Zen and the Art of Motorcycle Maintenance.* NY: 1974.

Poirier, Maurice. "Christopher Wilmarth: The Medium is Light", *Art News* (84:Dec. 1985), pp. 68-75.

Prebish, Charles S. *American Buddhism,* Duxbury Press, Mass. 1973.

Raffaele, Joe and Elizabeth Baker. "The Way-Out West: Interviews with Four San Francisco Artists", *Art News*, Summer 1967, p.40.

Raymond, Herbert. *Prince of Wizdumb: Herbert Raymond Looks at the Career of William Wiley, Art and Artists* (U.K.) Vol.8 Pt.8 (Nov 1973).

Read, Herbert. *Icon and Ideas.* NY: Schoken Books, 1965.

Reps, Paul. *Zen Flesh Zen Bones.* NY: Doubleday, n.d.

Rosen, Gerald. *Zen in the Art of J.D. Sallinger,* Creative Arts Book Co. Berkely, CA 1977.

Rosenberg, Harold. *The De-definition of Art.* NY: Horizon Press, 1972.

Ross, Nancy Wilson. *The World of Zen.* N.Y.: Vintage Books, 1960.

Rublowsky. *Pop Art,* Basic Books, NY 1965.

Sakanishi, Shio. *The Spirit of the Brush,* London 1939 (..Especially mentioned by Pearlstein and Baldessari).

Sasaki, Ruth Fuller and Isshu Miura. *Zen Dust,* The First Zen Institute of America in Japan, Kyoto, 1966.

Schwarz, H. Art and Photography: *Forerunners and Influences,* Gobson Smith, Inc. NY 1985.

Sharp, Willoughby. "New Direction in So. Cal. Sculpture". *Arts Magazine.* Vol.44, Summer 1970, pp.35-38.

Simon, Joan. "Breaking the Silence", *Art In America,* 76 (September, 1988), p. 142.

Smith, Brydon. *James Rosenquist,* National Gallery of Canada, 1968.

Snyder, Gary. *An Essay in Socially Engaged Buddhism in America* 1989.

Streng, F.J. *Emptiness:A Study in Religious Meaning,* Nashville, Abingdon Press, 1967.

Sullivan, Michael. *The Meeting of Eastern and Western Art,* London, 1973, The Arts of China University of California Press, 1977.

Suzuki, D. T. *Zen and Japanese Culture.* London: 1962.

Suzuki, Shunryu. *The Way of Zen. NY: Weatherhill,* 1970.

Tuchman, Maurice. *American Sculpture of the 60's.* (April 28-June 25, 1967) LA: LA County Museum, 1967.

Tuchman, Maurice. *The Spiritual in Art: Abstract Painting 1980-1985.* LA County Museum of Art NY: Abbeville Press, 1986.

Tucker, Marcia. *Bruce Nauman: Work From 1965-1972.* NY: Praeger Pub., 1972.

Tytell, John. "The Beat Generation and the Continuing American Revolution", *The American Scholar* vol. 4212, 1973 pp. 308-17.

Van Bruggen, Coosje. "Entrance, Entrapment, Exit", *Artforum,* 24 (Summer, 1986), p.88.

Waldman, Diane. *Michael Singer,* NY: Guggenheim Museum, 1984.

Waley, A. *Zen Buddhism and Its Relation to Art.* London, 1922.

Watts, Alan. *Beat Zen, Square Zen and Zen.* City Lights Books, San Francisco, 1959.

Watts, Alan. *The Spirit of Zen.* London: J. Murray, 1958.

Watts, Alan. *Zen Buddhism,* London: Buddhist Society, 1947.

Watts, Alan. *The Wisdom of Insecurity,* 1951. NY: Vintage Books.

Watts, Alan. *The Way of Zen,* NY: Random House, 1957.

Watts, Alan. *Psychotherapy East and West,* 1961. NY: Random House.

Watts, Alan. *The Book: On the Taboo Against Knowing Who You Are,* NY: Random House, 1966.

Weinpaul, Paul. "Zen and the Work of Wittgenstein", in *Chicago Review,* Vol. 12, No.2, 1958.

Welch, Lew. *I Remain: The Letters of Lew Welch and the Correspondence of His Friends,* two Volumes, Bolinas, Calif.

Weschler, Lawrence. *Seeing is Forgetting the Name of the Thing one Sees; The Life of Irwin.* Berkeley: U. of California Press, 1982.

Whiles, V. "Tantric Imagery—Affinities with 20thC Abstract Art". *Studio International,* March, 1971.

Wilhelm, Richard tr. *I Ching or Book of Changes,* London 1951.

Wilhelm, Richard tr. *The Secret of the Golden Flower,* (Commentary by C.G. Jung) originally tr. 1938.

Wilmarth, *Nine clearings for a standing man* (Hartford: Wadsworth Athenaeum 1974).

Wilson, John Oliver. *After Affluence.* San Fran 1980.

Yee, Chiang. *The Chinese Eye,* London 1935.

Young, Shinzen. "Stray Thoughts on Meditation", *Community Meditation Center,* Los Angeles, 1981.

Yu, Beongheon. *The Great Circle:American Writers and the Orient,* Wayne State University Press, Detroit, 1983.

# Glossary

ANATTA - "non -self", refers to the "self" as not changeless but as empty, negating the existence of Self. The idea that the identity of an individual is only a series of moments of consciousness.

ANICCA - "impermanence," all things in the samsara world. All things are transient, becoming, changing. Every effect has a cause and the cessation of effect is possible only by the cessation of the cause. There is no permanence in man's world.

CHI - material force, energy matter or substance, it explains physical form, individuality and the actuality of things. Chi is concrete and is often referred to as "breath," the inner energy, life force.

DHARMA - The wholly doctrine which contains (1) the final Reality; (2) correct order, virtue; (3) order of things; (4) by extension, the Universal Order, the Law; (5) perceptions grasped by the intellect.

I-CHING - A book about changes written by a Chinese monk who travelled in India (635-713) and left behind his ideas about life.

KOAN - An irrational statement for Zen meditation. It is meant to go beyond reason and logic and make an individual go deeper in order to reach Enlightenment, directing one's thoughts into one single issue.

MANDALA - "circle," a method of meditation which focuses on a visual chart or form, usually circular.

MAYA - illusion.

MU- "nothingness," a part of our essential self which is formless and found in all of of nature, such as the gaps and intervals between thoughts.

NIRVANA - Extinction or destruction of thirst or desire. Supreme state of Void, the goal of Buddhism consisting of the escape from the chain of births and deaths and the liberation from all effects of Karma. Also the real world as opposed to the illusory world of samasara.

PU - the Uncarved block, denoting the natural state of being, simplicity, purity and infinite potentiality.

SABI - the beauty of imperfection accompanied by antiquity or primitiveness, rustic unpretentiousness, simplicity, effortlessness, something rich in historical associations.

SATORI - Enlightenment, becoming a Buddha, ways of achieving this ultimate goal. Satori is "acquiring a new viewpoint." Satori is a state or mode of perception in which the habits of logical thinking, according to the rules of dualism, is destroyed. It is a new viewpoint for looking into the essence of reality. At the satori dimension, "All is one, one is none, none is all."

SUNYATA - the nothingness, the void and ultimately the world in a state of Sunya. Sunya is the void. In the state of being void or to be void. The goal in Buddhism is to become aware of and become one with the Void.

SUTRA - "thread," works supposedly containing the discourses of the Buddha or his immediate disciples. A spoken text which explains theories by metaphor or exposition. Expresses the main concepts of Buddhism.

TAI CHI - polarities of the universe.

TAO - "the Way," the great void that contains all energy.

TAOISM - Began in China based on TAO and a union of the real and ideal.

TAO TE CHING - The Book of the Way and all its virtues written supposedly by Lao Tzu.

TATHATA - "suchness," the Ultimate spiritual essence, things as they are in their own self nature.

YIN YANG - cyclical opposites, the polarity of forces against a background of the Void.

WABI - understatement.

WU WEI - "non-action," spontaneous and effortless actions, like a river or water which, of all things, is most yielding yet can overwhelm a rock which is, of all things, most hard.

ZEN - The Japanese pronunciation of Chan. Zen teaches salvation through enlightenment which is brought about by meditation. There is no objective Buddha to meditate on in Zen because one's own nature is Buddha. It relies on direct intuition. The techniques of Zen are Zazen, (sitting and meditating) and koan sanzen (questioning).